ARABIC

VOLUME 1
BEGINNERS AND
CHILDREN 8+

ARABIC LEARNING PROGRAM FOR NON - NATIVE SPEAKERS

LASMA SVIKE

Contents

بسم الله الرحمن الرحيم

This book covers:

- 74 past and present tense verbs divided based on root letters.
- Imperative form of verbs (expressing command)
- Nouns
- Verbal nouns
- Prepositions
- Question words
- Colours (masculine and feminine)
- Seasons
- Animals
- Adjectives (masculine and feminine)
- Body parts
- Cardinal numbers (1-10)
- Occupations
- Days of the week
- Gender of nouns (masculine and feminine)
- Singular pronouns
- Possessive pronouns (singular)
- Adjective + Noun (indefinite)
- Adjective + Noun (definite)
- Relationship between two nouns "Idaafah"
- Nominal sentence
- Expression "This is"
- Verb "to have" affirmative, negative, interrogative sentences and past form "had/didn't have"
- Adjective "every" (every day, every week, every month, every year)
- Adverbs (now, last night, yesterday, tomorrow)
- Simple sentences (practice of reading)

How to use the book

The Verb column* shows the 11 most common Arabic verbs forms and their 25 patterns

The darker tone indicates the pattern we study in the lesson

Red letters are to mark a difference in every pattern

Name of Arabic verbs form

A verbal noun is a noun derived from the verb, in some forms, there is no rule for deriving the verbal noun, as in this example, but if there is a certain rule, it will be marked in grey

Arabic verbs should be studied with their past and present tense together

The meaning of verbs, because *There is no infinitive form for Arabic verbs like to go, to open, or to do. In Arabic is used third person masculine*

Sentences to practice with verbs
The student reads the sentence and points to the verb and says it's past and present tense together

Verb column:

Triliteral
UNIT 1
ذَهَب / يَذْهَب
غَسَل / يَغْسِل
كَتَب / يَكْتُب
لَعِب / يَلْعَب

Triliteral with increase letters
UNIT 2
أَغْلَق / يُغْلِق
إِنْتَظَر / يَنْتَظِر
إِسْتَيْقَظ / يَسْتَيْقِظ

Triliteral with increase letters
UNIT 3
نَظَّف / يُنَظِّف
تَكَلَّم / يَتَكَلَّم
سَاعَد / يُسَاعِد

Assimilated
UNIT 4
وَضَع / يَضَع

Hollow
UNIT 5
قَال / يَقُول
بَاع / يَبِيع
نَام / يَنَام

Defective
UNIT 6
جَرى / يَجْري
نَسِيَ / يَنْسى
دَعا / يَدْعو

Defective
UNIT 7
صَلّى / يُصَلّي
أَعْطى / يُعْطي

Doubly week
UNIT 8
جَاءَ / يَجيءُ

Geminate
UNIT 9
عَدّ / يَعُدّ
أَحَبّ / يُحِبّ

Hamzated
UNIT 10
أَكَل / يَأْكُل

Hollow
UNIT 11
إِخْتَاز / يَخْتَار
أَجَاب / يُجيب

7

Study the first pattern of Thriliteral verbs carefully with their present and past tense together, make sure you know the meaning and verbal noun*

Thriliteral Arabic Verbs

verbal noun		present / past	
going	ذَهَاب	go	ذَهَب / يَذْهَب
opening	فَتْح	open	فَتَح / يَفْتَح
doing, verb	فَعَل	do	فَعَل / يَفْعَل

Note:
there is no infiniti~~ve~~ form for Arabic ve~~rbs~~ e.g., to go, to ope~~n~~ to do. In Arabic is used *third person masculine* e.g. Mohamed went
ذَهَب مُحَمَّد
Samir goes
يَذْهَب سَمير

To make the Imperative of Thriliteral verbs

- use present tense يَذْهَب
- remove the present tense prefix, in this case يَ and replace it with alif ا
- if the vowel on the second root letter is fatha or kasra, e.g. يَذْهَب (second root letter marked red) then the alif will take a kasrah
- if the vowel on the second root letter is damma, then the alif also take a damma

Read sentences, write, point on the verbs, say their past and present tense together

Sentences

ذَهَب أَحْمَدُ إِلَى الْمَلْعَبِ

فَتَح الْوَلَدُ الْبَابَ

مَاذَا يَفْعَلُ سَعيد؟

Study the Imperative form, used to say an order, command

Imperative verbs

masculine singular	Go!	إِذْهَب
feminine singular	Go!	إِذْهَبي
plural masculine	Go!	إِذْهَبُوا

To make the **masculine** *singular* Imperative remove the damma from the third root letter يَذْهَب (third root marked red) and put sukoon.
To make the **feminine** *singular* Imperative remove the damma from the third root letter يَذْهَب (third root marked red) and put kasrah and add ي
To make the **plural** *masculine* Imperative add و and silent alif ا

*Verbal noun is a noun derived from the verb.
There is no rule for deriving the verbal noun for Thriliteral Arabic Verbs

---

Forming an Imperative verb

The blue colour allows to read sentences properly

The Verb column works as a dictionary to easily find the verb pattern, its forming Imperative verb and its conjugation, which will be covered in Book 2

How to use the book

The Book consists of 11 UNITS covered in 25 lessons to allow a student to learn every lesson one pattern

LESSON 1   UNIT 1

Study the New words

Nouns			
house	بَيْتٌ	school	مَدْرَسَةٌ
boy	وَلَدٌ	playground	مَلْعَبٌ
girl	بِنْتٌ	writing board	سَبُّورَةٌ
window	نَافِذَةٌ	door	بَابٌ

New words to expand vocabulary. The Nouns are selected related to verbs, for example, open a door, window or to explain a new lesson, for example, this is a writing board

Study the Grammar lesson

feminine nouns	This is	masculine nouns	This is
مَدْرَسَةٌ this is a school	هَذِهِ	بَيْتٌ this is a house	هَذَا
نَافِذَةٌ this is a window	هَذِهِ	مَلْعَبٌ this is a playground	هَذَا
سَبُّورَةٌ this is a writing board	هَذِهِ	بَابٌ this is a door	هَذَا
بِنْتٌ this is a girl	هَذِهِ	وَلَدٌ this is a boy	هَذَا

Gender: all nouns in Arabic are either masculine الْمُذَكَّر or feminine الْمُؤَنَّث. Nearly all feminine words end with taa marbuta ة
There are words which are feminine by nature e.g., بِنْتٌ

This is:
هَذَا is used before masculine nouns
هَذِهِ is used before feminine nouns

Grammar lesson with colours to easily remember new rules

Note:
هَذَا is pronounced as هَاذَا
هَذِهِ is pronounced as هَاذِهِ

Study prepositions and question words

Prepositions		
ذَهَبَ سَمِيرٌ إِلَى الْمَدْرَسَةِ Samir went to the school	to	إِلَى

Question words		
مَاذَا يَفْعَلُ خَالِدٌ؟ What is Khalid doing?	what?	مَاذَا
هَذَا بَيْتٌ this is a house	what is this?	مَا هَذَا؟
هَذِهِ سَبُّورَةٌ this is a writing board	what is this?	مَا هَذِهِ؟

Prepositions, Question words or Adverbs with their sentences

6

*Study the **first** pattern of Thriliteral verbs carefully with their present and past tense together, make sure you know the meaning and verbal noun**

Thriliteral Arabic Verbs

verbal noun*			present / past
going	ذَهَابٌ	go	ذَهَبَ / يَذْهَبُ
opening	فَتْحٌ	open	فَتَحَ / يَفْتَحُ
doing, verb	فِعْلٌ	do	فَعَلَ / يَفْعَلُ

Note:
there is no infinitive form for Arabic verbs e.g., to go, to open, to do. In Arabic is used *third person masculine* e.g.
Mohamed went
ذَهَبَ مُحَمَّدٌ
Samir goes
يَذْهَبُ سَمِيرٌ

<u>To make the Imperative of Thriliteral verbs</u>

- use present tense يَذْهَبُ
- remove the present tense prefix, in this case يَ and replace it with alif ا
- if the vowel on the second root letter is fatha or kasra, e.g. يَذْهَبُ (second root letter marked red) then the alif will take a kasrah
- if the vowel on the second root letter is damma, then the alif will take a damma

Read sentences, write, point on the verbs, say their past and present tense together

Sentences

ذَهَبَ أَحْمَدُ إِلَى الْمَلْعَبِ.

فَتَحَ الْوَلَدُ الْبَابَ.

مَاذَا يَفْعَلُ سَعِيد؟

Study the Imperative form, used to say an order, command

Imperative verbs

masculine singular	Go!	اِذْهَبْ
feminine singular	Go!	اِذْهَبِي
plural masculine	Go!	اِذْهَبُوا

To make the **masculine** singular Imperative remove the damma from the third root letter يَذْهَبُ (third root letter marked red) and put sukoon.
To make the **feminine** singular Imperative remove the damma from the third root letter يَذْهَبُ (third root letter marked red) and put kasrah and add ي
To make the **plural masculine** Imperative add و and silent alif ا

*Verbal noun is a noun derived from the verb.
There is no rule for deriving the verbal noun for Thriliteral Arabic Verbs

Study the New words

Nouns

house	بَيْتٌ	school	مَدْرَسَةٌ
boy	وَلَدٌ	playground	مَلْعَبٌ
girl	بِنْتٌ	writing board	سَبُّورَةٌ
window	نَافِذَةٌ	door	بَابٌ

Study the Grammar lesson

feminine nouns	This is	masculine nouns	This is
مَدْرَسَةٌ	هَذِهِ	بَيْتٌ	هَذَا
this is a school		this is a house	
نَافِذَةٌ	هَذِهِ	مَلْعَبٌ	هَذَا
this is a window		this is a playground	
سَبُّورَةٌ	هَذِهِ	بَابٌ	هَذَا
this is a writing board		this is a door	
بِنْتٌ	هَذِهِ	وَلَدٌ	هَذَا
this is a girl		this is a boy	

Gender: all nouns in Arabic are either masculine الْمُذَكَّر or feminine الْمُؤَنَّث . Nearly all feminine words end with taa marbuta ة
There are words which are feminine by nature e.g., بِنْتٌ

This is:
هَذَا is used before masculine nouns
هَذِهِ is used before feminine nouns

Note:
هَذَا is pronounced as هَاذَا
هَذِهِ is pronounced as هَاذِهِ

Study prepositions and question words

Prepositions

	to	إِلَى
ذَهَبَ سَمِيرٌ إِلَى الْمَدْرَسَةِ.		
Samir went to the school		

Question words

	what?	مَاذَا
مَاذَا يَفْعَلُ خَالِدٌ؟		
What is Khalid doing?		
هَذَا بَيْتٌ.	what is this?	مَا هَذَا؟
this is a house		
هَذِهِ سَبُّورَةٌ.	what is this?	مَا هَذِهِ؟
this is a writing board		

Triliteral	UNIT 1
Triliteral with increase letters	UNIT 2
Triliteral with increase letters	UNIT 3
Assimilated	UNIT 4
Hollow	UNIT 5
Defective	UNIT 6
Defective	UNIT 7
Doubly week	UNIT 8
Geminate	UNIT 9
Hamzated	UNIT 10
Hollow	UNIT 11

Triliteral — UNIT 1

ذَهَبَ / يَذْهَبُ
غَسَلَ / يَغْسِلُ
كَتَبَ / يَكْتُبُ
لَعِبَ / يَلْعَبُ

Triliteral with increase letters — UNIT 2

أَغْلَقَ / يُغْلِقُ
اِنْتَظَرَ / يَنْتَظِرُ
اِسْتَيْقَظَ / يَسْتَيْقِظُ

Triliteral with increase letters — UNIT 3

نَظَّفَ / يُنَظِّفُ
تَكَلَّمَ / يَتَكَلَّمُ
سَاعَدَ / يُسَاعِدُ

Assimilated — UNIT 4

وَضَعَ / يَضَعُ

Hollow — UNIT 5

قَالَ / يَقُولُ
بَاعَ / يَبِيعُ
نَامَ / يَنَامُ

Defective — UNIT 6

جَرَى / يَجْرِي
نَسِيَ / يَنْسَى
دَعَا / يَدْعُو

Defective — UNIT 7

صَلَّى / يُصَلِّي
أَعْطَى / يُعْطِي

Doubly week — UNIT 8

جَاءَ / يَجِيءُ

Geminate — UNIT 9

عَدَّ / يَعُدُّ
أَحَبَّ / يُحِبُّ

Hamzated — UNIT 10

أَكَلَ / يَأْكُلُ

Hollow — UNIT 11

اِخْتَارَ / يَخْتَارُ
أَجَابَ / يُجِيبُ

---

*Study the **second** pattern of Thriliteral verbs carefully with their present and past tense together, make sure you know the meaning and verbal noun**

Thriliteral Arabic Verbs			
verbal noun*			present / past
washing	غَسْلٌ	wash	غَسَلَ / يَغْسِلُ
carrying	حَمْلٌ	carry	حَمَلَ / يَحْمِلُ
sitting	جُلُوسٌ	sit	جَلَسَ / يَجْلِسُ
going down	نُزُولٌ	go down, get off	نَزَلَ / يَنْزِلُ

Remember:
there is no infinitive form for Arabic verbs e.g., to wash, to do. In Arabic is used *third person masculine* e.g.
Mohamed washed
غَسَلَ مُحَمَّدٌ
Samir sits
يَجْلِسُ سَمِيرٌ

Read sentences, write, point on the verbs, say their past and present tense together

Sentences
هُوَ يَغْسِلُ الْمَلَابِسَ.
يَحْمِلُ مُحَمَّدٌ حَقِيبَةً.
هُوَ يَجْلِسُ عَلَى الْكُرْسِيِّ.
نَزَلَ التِّلْمِيذُ مِنَ الْحَافِلَةِ.
أَيْنَ الْكِتَابُ؟ هُوَ فِي الْحَقِيبَةِ.
هُوَ يَحْمِلُ كِتَابًا.

To make the Imperative
follow the same rules of first pattern Thiriliteral verbs

Study the Imperative form, used to say an order, command

Imperative verbs		
masculine *singular*	Wash!	اِغْسِلْ
feminine *singular*	Wash!	اِغْسِلِي
plural *masculine*	Wash!	اِغْسِلُوا

Remember:
if the vowel on the second root letter is fatha or kasrah, e.g.,
يَغْسِلُ *(second root letter marked red)*
then the alif will take a kasrah

*Verbal noun is a noun derived from the verb.
There is no rule for deriving the verbal noun for Thriliteral Arabic Verbs

8

Study the New words

Nouns

bag	حَقِيبَةٌ	clothes	مَلَابِسٌ
chair	كُرْسِيٌّ	bus	حَافِلَةٌ
pupil	تِلْمِيذٌ	book	كِتَابٌ
car	سَيَّارَةٌ	park	حَدِيقَةٌ

Study the Grammar lesson

Pronouns (singular)

he			هُوَ
she			هِيَ
I			أَنَا
you (speak with male)			أَنْتَ
you (speak with female)			أَنْتِ
it	هِيَ feminine words	or	هُوَ masculine words

Note:
there is no word
it in Arabic, all
nouns are referred
to as he or she

Study prepositions and question words

Question words

أَيْنَ الْحَقِيبَةُ؟	where?	أَيْنَ
Where is the bag?		

Prepositions

هِيَ عَلَى الْكُرْسِيِّ.	on	عَلَى
It is on the chair		
الْوَلَدُ فِي الْحَدِيقَةِ.	in	فِي
The boy is in the park		

*Study the **third** pattern of Thriliteral verbs carefully with their present and past tense together, make sure you know the meaning and verbal noun**

Thriliteral Arabic Verbs

verbal noun*			present / past
writing	كِتَابَةٌ	write	كَتَبَ / يَكْتُبُ
exit	خُرُوجٌ	exit, go out	خَرَجَ / يَخْرُجُ
entering	دُخُولٌ	enter, go inside	دَخَلَ / يَدْخُلُ
living	سَكَنٌ	live	سَكَنَ / يَسْكُنُ

Read sentences, write, point on the verbs, say their past and present tense together

Sentences

يَكْتُبُ بِلَالٌ رِسَالَةً.

خَرَجَ مُحَمَّدٌ مِنَ الْبَيْتِ.

دَخَلَ التِّلْمِيذُ إِلَى الصَّفِّ.

هُوَ يَسْكُنُ قَرِيبًا مِنَ الْمَدْرَسَةِ.

دَخَلَ الْوَلَدُ إِلَى الْبَيْتِ.

هُوَ يَكْتُبُ عَلَى الْوَرَقَةِ.

To make the Imperative follow the same rules of first pattern Thriliteral verbs

Study the Imperative form, used to say an order, command

Imperative verbs

masculine singular	Write!	اُكْتُبْ
feminine singular	Write!	اُكْتُبِي
plural masculine	Write!	اُكْتُبُوا

Remember:

if the vowel on the second root letter is damma, يَكْتُبُ (second root letter marked red) then the alif will also take a damma

*Verbal noun is a noun derived from the verb.
There is no rule for deriving the verbal noun for Thriliteral Arabic Verbs

Study the New words

Nouns

pen	قَلَمٌ	paper	وَرَقَةٌ
class	صَفٌّ	letter	رِسَالَةٌ
room	غُرْفَةٌ	notebook	كُرَّاسَةٌ

Study prepositions

Prepositions

هُوَ خَرَجَ مَعَ الْوَلَدِ. He went out with the boy	with (human)	مَعَ
هُوَ يَكْتُبُ بِالْقَلَمِ. He writes with the pen	with (things)	بِ
هُوَ يَسْكُنُ قَرِيبًا مِنَ الْمَدْرَسَةِ. He lives near the school	near	قَرِيب
هُوَ يَسْكُنُ بَعِيدًا عَنِ الْمَدْرَسَةِ. He lives far from the school	far	بَعِيد
خَرَجَ سَمِيرٌ مِنَ الْغُرْفَةِ. Samir went out from the room	from	مِنْ

Remember: the noun coming immediately after preposition ends with kasrah

Note: when the preposition مِنْ is followed by a word with definite article al, the sukun is changed to fatha, to ease pronunciation

Triliteral

ذَهَبَ / يَذْهَبُ

غَسَلَ / يَغْسِلُ

كَتَبَ / يَكْتُبُ

لَعِبَ / يَلْعَبُ

UNIT 1

*Study the **fourth** pattern of Thriliteral verbs carefully with their present and past tense together, make sure you know the meaning and verbal noun**

Thriliteral Arabic Verbs

verbal noun*			present / past
playing	لَعِبٌ	play	لَعِبَ / يَلْعَبُ
drinking	شُرْبٌ	drink	شَرِبَ / يَشْرَبُ
wearing	لُبْسٌ	wear, put on	لَبِسَ / يَلْبَسُ
riding	رُكُوبٌ	ride, get on	رَكِبَ / يَرْكَبُ

Read sentences, write, point on the verbs, say their past and present tense together

<u>To make the Imperative</u> follow the same rules of first pattern Thiriliteral verbs

Sentences

يَلْعَبُ مُنِيرٌ بِلُعْبَتِي .

يَشْرَبُ عَلِيٌّ حَلِيبًا .

يَلْبَسُ كَمَالٌ قَمِيصًا .

يَرْكَبُ مُحَمَّدٌ حَافِلَةً .

هُوَ يَشْرَبُ مَاءً .

يَرْكَبُ بِلَالٌ دَرَّاجَتِي .

Study the Imperative form, used to say an order, command

Imperative verbs

masculine *singular*	Play!	اِلْعَبْ
feminine *singular*	Play!	اِلْعَبِي
plural *masculine*	Play!	اِلْعَبُوا

<u>Remember:</u>
if the vowel on the second root letter is fatha or kasrah, e.g., يَلْعَبُ (second root letter marked red) then the alif will take a kasrah

*Verbal noun is a noun derived from the verb.
There is no rule for deriving the verbal noun for Thriliteral Arabic Verbs

Study the New words

Nouns

milk	حَلِيبٌ	bicycle	دَرَّاجَةٌ
father	أَبٌ	shirt	قَمِيصٌ
mother	أُمٌّ	toy, game	لُعْبَةٌ
		water	مَاءٌ

Study the Grammar lesson

My

my book	كِتَابِي	كِتَابٌ
my house	بَيْتِي	بَيْتٌ
my toy	لُعْبَتِي	لُعْبَةٌ
my bicycle	دَرَّاجَتِي	دَرَّاجَةٌ
my mother	أُمِّي	أُمٌّ
my pen	قَلَمِي	قَلَمٌ

Possessive pronoun: **my**

In Arabic possessive pronouns e.g., my, yours, his, her etc. are not words, but they are like suffixes attached to the ending of the nouns.

As we can see "my book" is كِتَابِي

Study question words

Question words

هَذَا وَلَدٌ.	who is this?	مَنْ هَذَا؟
this is a boy		
هَذِهِ أُمِّي.	who is this?	مَنْ هَذِهِ؟
this is my mother		

Triliteral

ذَهَبَ / يَذْهَبُ
غَسَلَ / يَغْسِلُ
كَتَبَ / يَكْتُبُ
لَعِبَ / يَلْعَبُ

UNIT 1

Triliteral with
increase letters

أَغْلَقَ / يُغْلِقُ
اِنْتَظَرَ / يَنْتَظِرُ
اِسْتَيْقَظَ / يَسْتَيْقِظُ

UNIT 2

Triliteral with
increase letters

نَظَّفَ / يُنَظِّفُ
تَكَلَّمَ / يَتَكَلَّمُ
سَاعَدَ / يُسَاعِدُ

UNIT 3

Assimilated

وَضَعَ / يَضَعُ

UNIT 4

Hollow

قَالَ / يَقُولُ
بَاعَ / يَبِيعُ
نَامَ / يَنَامُ

UNIT 5

Defective

جَرَى / يَجْرِي
نَسِيَ / يَنْسَى
دَعَا / يَدْعُو

UNIT 6

Defective

صَلَّى / يُصَلِّي
أَعْطَى / يُعْطِي

UNIT 7

Doubly week

جَاءَ / يَجِيءُ

UNIT 8

Geminate

عَدَّ / يَعُدُّ
أَحَبَّ / يُحِبُّ

UNIT 9

Hamzated

أَكَلَ / يَأْكُلُ

UNIT 10

Hollow

اِخْتَارَ / يَخْتَارُ
أَجَابَ / يُجِيبُ

UNIT 11

*Study the pattern of Thriliteral verbs with **one increase letter** carefully with their present and past tense together, make sure you know the meaning and verbal noun**

Thriliteral Arabic Verbs with one increase letter

verbal noun*			present / past
closing	إِغْلَاقٌ	close	أَغْلَقَ / يُغْلِقُ
catching	إِمْسَاكٌ	catch, hold	أَمْسَكَ / يُمْسِكُ
finishing	إِكْمَالٌ	finish, complete	أَكْمَلَ / يُكْمِلُ

Read sentences, write, point on the verbs, say their past and present tense together

Sentences

هُوَ أَغْلَقَ الْبَابَ.

أَمْسَكَ الْوَلَدُ الْكُرَةَ.

أَكْمَلَ بِلَالٌ الْوَاجِبَ.

أَغْلِقْ النَّافِذَةَ.

أَيْنَ كِتَابُكَ؟ هُوَ فِي الْحَقِيبَةِ.

أَيْنَ أُمُّكَ؟ هِيَ فِي الْبَيْتِ.

Study the Imperative form, used to say an order, command

Imperative verbs

masculine *singular*	Close!	أَغْلِقْ
feminine *singular*	Close!	أَغْلِقِي
plural *masculine*	Close!	أَغْلِقُوا

To make the Imperative:

- use present tense يُغْلِقُ
- remove the present tense prefix, in this case يُ and replace it with alif ا with fatha أَ
- follow the rules of making masculine (singular), feminine (singular) and plural (masculine) Imperative

*Verbal noun is a noun derived from the verb.
There is a rule for deriving the verbal noun from this pattern. Verbal noun are made by following pattern إِفْعَالٌ

14

Study the New words

Nouns

bridge	جِسْرٌ	table	طَاوِلَةٌ
car	سَيَّارَةٌ	homework	وَاجِبٌ
lesson	دَرْسٌ	ball	كُرَةٌ
		street	شَارِعٌ

Study the Grammar lesson

Your (speak with male)

your pen	قَلَمُكَ	قَلَمٌ
your book	كِتَابُكَ	كِتَابٌ
your ball	كُرَتُكَ	كُرَةٌ
your car	سَيَّارَتُكَ	سَيَّارَةٌ
your chair	كُرْسِيُّكَ	كُرْسِيٌّ

Possessive pronoun:
your

In Arabic possessive pronouns e.g., my, yours, his, her etc. are not words, but they are like suffixes attached to the ending of the nouns.

As we can see "your book" is كِتَابُكَ

Note: there is difference in Arabic when speaking with male or female, if we speak with male, we use suffix كَ when speak with female we use suffix كِ

Study prepositions

Prepositions

الكُرَةُ تَحْتَ الطَّاوِلَةِ.	under	تَحْتَ
The ball is under the table		
السَّيَّارَةُ فَوْقَ الْجِسْرِ.	on, over, above	فَوْقَ
The car is on the bridge		

Remember:
the noun coming immediately after preposition ends with kasrah

*Study the pattern of Thriliteral verbs with **two increase letters** carefully with their present and past tense together, make sure you know the meaning and verbal noun**

Thriliteral Arabic Verbs with **two** increase letters			
verbal noun*			present / past
waiting	اِنْتِظَارٌ	wait	اِنْتَظَرَ / يَنْتَظِرِ
smile	اِبْتِسَامٌ	smile	اِبْتَسَمَ / يَبْتَسِمُ
working hard	اِجْتِهَادٌ	work hard	اِجْتَهَدَ / يَجْتَهِدُ

Read sentences, write, point on the verbs, say their past and present tense together

Sentences
يَنْتَظِرُ سَمِيرٌ الْأَصْدِقَاءَ.
يَجْتَهِدُ بِلَالٌ فِي الدُّرُوسِ.
يَنْتَظِرُ أَحْمَدُ حَافِلَةً.
اِبْتَسَمَ صَدِيقِي.
اِجْتَهِدِي فِي الدُّرُوسِ.
مِنْ أَيْنَ أَنْتَ؟ أَنَا مِنْ أَمْرِيكَا.

Study the Imperative form, used to say an order, command

Imperative verbs		
masculine *singular*	Wait!	اِنْتَظِرْ
feminine *singular*	Wait!	اِنْتَظِرِي
plural *masculine*	Wait!	اِنْتَظِرُوا

<u>To make the Imperative:</u>

- use present tense يَنْتَظِرُ
- remove the present tense prefix, in this case يَ and replace it with alif ا with kasrah اِ
- follow the rules of making masculine (singular), feminine (singular) and plural (masculine) Imperative

*Verbal noun is a noun derived from the verb.

There is a rule for deriving the verbal noun from this pattern. Verbal noun are made by following pattern اِفْتِعَالٌ

16

Study the New words

Nouns

friends	أَصْدِقَاء	name	اِسْمٌ
man	رَجُلٌ	lessons	دُرُوس
son	اِبْنٌ	teacher	مُعَلِّمٌ
		friend	صَدِيقٌ

Study the Grammar lesson

Your (speak with female)

your pen	قَلَمُكِ	قَلَمٌ
your book	كِتَابُكِ	كِتَابٌ
your ball	كُرَتُكِ	كُرَةٌ
your car	سَيَّارَتُكِ	سَيَّارَةٌ
your chair	كُرْسِيُّكِ	كُرْسِيٌّ

Remember: there is difference in Arabic when speaking with male or female, if we speak with male, we use suffix كَ when speak with female we use suffix كِ

Study the prepositions and question words

Prepositions

	from	مِن
أَنَا مِنْ إِيرْلَنْدَا.		
I am from Ireland		

Question words

	what?	مَا
مَا اسْمُكِ؟		
What is your name?		
(speak with female)		

Note: see list of countries in Arabic at the end of the book

Note: the words اِسْمٌ and اِبْنٌ start with hamzatu l- wasl. When preceded by a word the ا is dropped in pronunciation
اِسْمُ الْوَلَدِ مُحَمَّدٌ،
وَاسْمُ الْبِنْتِ فَاطِمَةُ

UNIT 1
UNIT 2
UNIT 3
UNIT 4
UNIT 5
UNIT 6
UNIT 7
UNIT 8
UNIT 9
UNIT 10
UNIT 11

Triliteral

ذَهَبَ / يَذْهَبُ
غَسَلَ / يَغْسِلُ
كَتَبَ / يَكْتُبُ
لَعِبَ / يَلْعَبُ

Triliteral with increase letters

أَغْلَقَ / يُغْلِقُ
اِنْتَظَرَ / يَنْتَظِرُ
اِسْتَيْقَظَ / يَسْتَيْقِظُ

Triliteral with increase letters

نَظَّفَ / يُنَظِّفُ
تَكَلَّمَ / يَتَكَلَّمُ
سَاعَدَ / يُسَاعِدُ

Assimilated

وَضَعَ / يَضَعُ

Hollow

قَالَ / يَقُولُ
بَاعَ / يَبِيعُ
نَامَ / يَنَامُ

Defective

جَرَى / يَجْرِي
نَسِيَ / يَنْسَى
دَعَا / يَدْعُو

Defective

صَلَّى / يُصَلِّي
أَعْطَى / يُعْطِي

Doubly week

جَاءَ / يَجِيءُ

Geminate

عَدَّ / يَعُدُّ
أَحَبَّ / يُحِبُّ

Hamzated

أَكَلَ / يَأْكُلُ

Hollow

اِخْتَارَ / يَخْتَارُ
أَجَابَ / يُجِيبُ

---

*Study the pattern of Thriliteral verbs with **three increase letters** carefully with their present and past tense together, make sure you know the meaning and verbal noun**

Thriliteral Arabic Verbs with *three* increase letters			
verbal noun*			present / past
waking up	اِسْتِيْقَاظٌ	wake up	اِسْتَيْقَظَ / يَسْتَيْقِظُ
welcoming	اِسْتِقْبَالٌ	welcome	اِسْتَقْبَلَ / يَسْتَقْبِلُ
using	اِسْتِعْمَالٌ	use	اِسْتَعْمَلَ / يَسْتَعْمِلُ

Read sentences, write, point on the verbs, say their past and present tense together

Sentences
يَسْتَيْقِظُ عَبْدُ اللَّهِ مُبَكِّرًا.
اِسْتَقْبَلَ الْمُعَلِّمُ التَّلَامِيذَ.
اِسْتَعْمَلَ بَشِيرٌ الْقَلَمَ الْأَحْمَرَ.
اِسْتَيْقَظَ أَخِي مُتَأَخِّرًا.
هَذِهِ الْكُرَةُ زَرْقَاءُ.
هَذَا الْبَيْتُ أَبْيَضُ.

Study the Imperative form, used to say an order, command

Imperative verbs		
masculine *singular*	Wake up!	اِسْتَيْقِظْ
feminine *singular*	Wake up!	اِسْتَيْقِظِي
plural *masculine*	Wake up!	اِسْتَيْقِظُوا

<u>To make the Imperative:</u>
- use present tense يَسْتَيْقِظُ
- remove the present tense prefix, in this case يَ and replace it with alif ا with kasrah اِ
- follow the rules of making masculine (*singular*), feminine (*singular*) and plural (*masculine*) Imperative

*Verbal noun is a noun derived from the verb.
There is a rule for deriving the verbal noun from this pattern. Verbal noun are made by following pattern اِسْتِفْعَالٌ

Study the New words

Nouns

pupil	تِلْمِيذٌ	word	كَلِمَةٌ
pupils	تَلَامِيذ	sentence	جُمْلَةٌ
brother	أَخٌ	early	مُبَكِّرًا
colour	لَوْنٌ	late	مُتَأَخِّرًا

Learn the colours in Arabic

Colours

	feminine	masculine
blue	زَرْقَاءُ	أَزْرَقُ
black	سَوْدَاءُ	أَسْوَدُ
red	حَمْرَاءُ	أَحْمَرُ
yellow	صَفْرَاءُ	أَصْفَرُ
white	بَيْضَاءُ	أَبْيَضُ
green	خَضْرَاءُ	أَخْضَرُ

Colours: colours in Arabic have masculine and feminine forms. When a noun is masculine, the colour describing it will also be masculine. Likewise, when a noun is feminine, the colour describing it will also be feminine

أَيْنَ الْحَافِلَةُ الصَّفْرَاءُ؟

أَيْنَ الْقَلَمُ الْأَخْضَرُ؟

Exceptions with words father and brother

your brother	أَخُوك	أَخٌ
your father	أَبُوك	أَبٌ

19

Triliteral	UNIT 1
ذَهَبَ / يَذْهَبُ	
غَسَلَ / يَغْسِلُ	
كَتَبَ / يَكْتُبُ	
لَعِبَ / يَلْعَبُ	
Triliteral with increase letters	UNIT 2
أَغْلَقَ / يُغْلِقُ	
إِنْتَظَرَ / يَنْتَظِرُ	
إِسْتَيْقَظَ / يَسْتَيْقِظُ	
Triliteral with increase letters	UNIT 3
نَظَّفَ / يُنَظِّف	
تَكَلَّمَ / يَتَكَلَّمُ	
سَاعَدَ / يُسَاعِدُ	
Assimilated	UNIT 4
وَضَعَ / يَضَعُ	
Hollow	UNIT 5
قَالَ / يَقُولُ	
بَاعَ / يَبِيعُ	
نَامَ / يَنَامُ	
Defective	UNIT 6
جَرَى / يَجْرِي	
نَسِيَ / يَنْسَى	
دَعَا / يَدْعُو	
Defective	UNIT 7
صَلَّى / يُصَلِّي	
أَعْطَى / يُعْطِي	
Doubly week	UNIT 8
جَاءَ / يَجِيءُ	
Geminate	UNIT 9
عَدَّ / يَعُدُّ	
أَحَبَّ / يُحِبُّ	
Hamzated	UNIT 10
أَكَلَ / يَأْكُلُ	
Hollow	UNIT 11
إِخْتَارَ / يَخْتَارُ	
أَجَابَ / يُجِيبُ	

*Study the pattern of Thriliteral verbs with **increase letters** carefully with their present and past tense together, make sure you know the meaning and verbal noun**

Thriliteral Arabic Verbs with increase letters

verbal noun*			present / past
cleaning	تَنْظِيفٌ	clean	نَظَّفَ / يُنَظِّفُ
arranging	تَرْتِيبٌ	organize, arrange	رَتَّبَ / يُرَتِّبُ
thinking	تَفْكِيرٌ	think	فَكَّرَ / يُفَكِّرُ

Read sentences, write, point on the verbs, say their past and present tense together

Sentences

يُنَظِّفُ سَلِيمٌ أَسْنَانَهُ.

هُوَ يُرَتِّبُ حَقِيبَتَهُ.

فَكَّرَ حَسَنٌ فِي الذَّهَابِ إِلَى الْحَدِيقَةِ.

نَظِّفْ أَسْنَانَكَ.

رَتِّبِي غُرْفَتَكِ.

أَيْنَ كُرَتُهُ؟ هِيَ وَرَاءَ الشَّجَرَةِ.

Study the Imperative form, used to say an order, command

Imperative verbs

masculine *singular*	Clean!	نَظِّفْ
feminine *singular*	Clean!	نَظِّفِي
plural *masculine*	Clean!	نَظِّفُوا

<u>To make the Imperative:</u>

• use present tense يُنَظِّفُ
• remove the present tense prefix, in this case يُ
• follow the rules of making masculine (singular), feminine (singular) and plural (masculine) Imperative

*Verbal noun is a noun derived from the verb.
There is a rule for deriving the verbal noun from this pattern. Verbal noun are made by following pattern تَفْعِيلٌ

Study the New words

Nouns

tooth	سِنٌّ	gift	هَدِيَّةٌ
teeth	أَسْنَانٌ	box	صُنْدُوقٌ
tree	شَجَرَةٌ	holiday	عُطْلَةٌ

Study the Grammar lesson

His

his pen	قَلَمُهُ	قَلَمٌ
his book	كِتَابُهُ	كِتَابٌ
his ball	كُرَتُهُ	كُرَةٌ
his car	سَيَّارَتُهُ	سَيَّارَةٌ
his chair	كُرْسِيُّهُ	كُرْسِيٌّ

Possessive pronoun: **his**

In Arabic possessive pronouns e.g., *my, yours, his, her* etc. are not words, but they are like suffixes attached to the ending of the nouns.

As we can see "his book" is كِتَابُهُ

Study the prepositions

Prepositions

الكُرَةُ أَمَامَ الصُّنْدُوقِ.	in front of	أَمَامَ
The ball is in front of the box		
الكُرَةُ وَرَاءَ الصُّنْدُوقِ.	behind	وَرَاءَ
The ball is behind the box		
البَيْتُ خَلْفَ المَدْرَسَةِ.	behind	خَلْفَ
The house is behind the school		

Triliteral

ذَهَبَ / يَذْهَبُ
غَسَلَ / يَغْسِلُ
كَتَبَ / يَكْتُبُ
لَعِبَ / يَلْعَبُ

UNIT 1

Triliteral with increase letters

أَغْلَقَ / يُغْلِقُ
اِنْتَظَرَ / يَنْتَظِرُ
اِسْتَيْقَظَ / يَسْتَيْقِظُ

UNIT 2

Triliteral with increase letters

نَظَّفَ / يُنَظِّفُ
تَكَلَّمَ / يَتَكَلَّمُ
سَاعَدَ / يُسَاعِدُ

UNIT 3

Assimilated

وَضَعَ / يَضَعُ

UNIT 4

Hollow

قَالَ / يَقُول
بَاعَ / يَبِيعُ
نَامَ / يَنَامُ

UNIT 5

Defective

جَرَى / يَجْرِي
نَسِيَ / يَنْسَى
دَعَا / يَدْعُو

UNIT 6

Defective

صَلَّى / يُصَلِّي
أَعْطَى / يُعْطِي

UNIT 7

Doubly week

جَاءَ / يَجِيءُ

UNIT 8

Geminate

عَدَّ / يَعُدُّ
أَحَبَّ / يُحِبُّ

UNIT 9

Hamzated

أَكَلَ / يَأْكُلُ

UNIT 10

Hollow

اِخْتَارَ / يَخْتَارُ
أَجَابَ / يُجِيبُ

UNIT 11

*Study the pattern of Thriliteral verbs with **increase letters** carefully with their present and past tense together, make sure you know the meaning and verbal noun**

Thriliteral Arabic Verbs with increase letters

verbal noun*			present / past
speaking	تَكَلُّمٌ	speak	تَكَلَّمَ / يَتَكَلَّمُ
learning	تَعَلُّمٌ	learn	تَعَلَّمَ / يَتَعَلَّمُ
stopping	تَوَقُّفٌ	stop	تَوَقَّفَ / يَتَوَقَّفُ

Read sentences, write, point on the verbs, say their past and present tense together

Sentences

هُوَ يَتَكَلَّمُ اللُّغَةَ الْعَرَبِيَّةَ.

يَتَعَلَّمُ التِّلْمِيذُ الْقِرَاءَةَ وَالْكِتَابَةَ فِي الْمَدْرَسَةِ.

تَوَقَّفَ الْوَلَدُ أَمَامَ الْمَدْرَسَةِ.

تَكَلَّمْ مَعَ الْمُعَلِّمِ بِاللُّغَةِ الْعَرَبِيَّةِ.

تَوَقَّفْ عِنْدَ الشَّجَرَةِ.

أَيْنَ قَلَمُهَا؟ هُوَ عَلَى الْمَكْتَبِ.

Study the Imperative form, used to say an order, command

Imperative verbs

masculine singular	Speak!	تَكَلَّمْ
feminine singular	Speak!	تَكَلَّمِي
plural masculine	Speak!	تَكَلَّمُوا

To make the Imperative:

- use present tense يَتَكَلَّمُ
- remove the present tense prefix, in this case يَ
- follow the rules of making masculine (singular), feminine (singular) and plural (masculine) Imperative

*Verbal noun is a noun derived from the verb.
There is a rule for deriving the verbal noun from this pattern. Verbal noun are made by following pattern تَفَعُّلٌ

Study the New words

Nouns

Arabic language	اللُّغَةُ الْعَرَبِيَّة	reading	قِرَاءَةٌ
desk	مَكْتَبٌ	writing	كِتَابَةٌ
library	مَكْتَبَةٌ	language	لُغَةٌ

Study the Grammar lesson

Her

her pen	قَلَمُهَا	قَلَمٌ
her book	كِتَابُهَا	كِتَابٌ
her ball	كُرَتُهَا	كُرَةٌ
her car	سَيَّارَتُهَا	سَيَّارَةٌ
her chair	كُرْسِيُّهَا	كُرْسِيٌّ

*Possessive pronoun: **her***

In Arabic possessive pronouns e.g., my, yours, his, her etc. are not words, but they are like suffixes attached to the ending of the nouns.

As we can see "her book" is كِتَابُهَا

Study the adjectives

Adjectives

هُوَ يَتَكَلَّمُ اللُّغَةَ الْعَرَبِيَّةَ قَلِيلًا. He speaks Arabic little	few, little	قَلِيل
يَتَكَلَّمُ سَمِيرٌ كَثِيرًا. Samir speaks too much	many, too much	كَثِير

Triliteral	UNIT 1
ذَهَبَ / يَذْهَبُ	
غَسَلَ / يَغْسِلُ	
كَتَبَ / يَكْتُبُ	
لَعِبَ / يَلْعَبُ	
Triliteral with increase letters	UNIT 2
أَغْلَقَ / يُغْلِقُ	
اِنْتَظَرَ / يَنْتَظِرُ	
اِسْتَيْقَظَ / يَسْتَيْقِظُ	
Triliteral with increase letters	UNIT 3
نَظَّفَ / يُنَظِّفُ	
تَكَلَّمَ / يَتَكَلَّمُ	
سَاعَدَ / يُسَاعِدُ	
Assimilated	UNIT 4
وَضَعَ / يَضَعُ	
Hollow	UNIT 5
قَالَ / يَقُول	
بَاعَ / يَبِيعُ	
نَامَ / يَنَامُ	
Defective	UNIT 6
جَرَى / يَجْرِي	
نَسِيَ / يَنْسَى	
دَعَا / يَدْعُو	
Defective	UNIT 7
صَلَّى / يُصَلِّي	
أَعْطَى / يُعْطِي	
Doubly week	UNIT 8
جَاءَ / يَجِيءُ	
Geminate	UNIT 9
عَدَّ / يَعُدُّ	
أَحَبَّ / يُحِبُّ	
Hamzated	UNIT 10
أَكَلَ / يَأْكُلُ	
Hollow	UNIT 11
اِخْتَارَ / يَخْتَارُ	
أَجَابَ / يُجِيبُ	

*Study the pattern of Thriliteral verbs with **increase letters** carefully with their present and past tense together, make sure you know the meaning and verbal noun**

Thriliteral Arabic Verbs with increase letters

verbal noun*			present / past
help	مُسَاعَدَةٌ	help	سَاعَدَ / يُسَاعِدُ
revision	مُرَاجَعَةٌ	revise	رَاجَعَ / يُرَاجِعُ
traveling	مُسَافَرَةٌ	travel	سَافَرَ / يُسَافِرُ

Read sentences, write, point on the verbs, say their past and present tense together

Sentences

سَاعَدَ مُنِيرٌ صَدِيقَهُ.

يُرَاجِعُ بِلَالٌ دُرُوسَهُ.

سَافَرَ أَبِي مَعَ أَخِي إِلَى الْمَدِينَةِ بِالْقِطَارِ.

سَاعَدَ الْمُعَلِّمُ التَّلَامِيذَ.

رَاجِعْ سُورَةَ الرَّحْمَانِ.

سَافَرَ عَلِيٌّ بِالطَّائِرَةِ.

Study the Imperative form, used to say an order, command

Imperative verbs

masculine singular	Help!	سَاعِدْ
feminine singular	Help!	سَاعِدِي
plural masculine	Help!	سَاعِدُوا

To make the Imperative:
- use present tense يُسَاعِدُ
- remove the present tense prefix, in this case يُ
- follow the rules of making masculine (*singular*), feminine (*singular*) and plural (*masculine*) Imperative

*Verbal noun is a noun derived from the verb.
There is a rule for deriving the verbal noun from this pattern. Verbal noun are made by following pattern مُفَاعَلَةٌ

Study the New words

Nouns

train	قِطَارٌ	country	بَلَدٌ
airplane	طَائِرَةٌ	city	مَدِينَةٌ
books	كُتُبٌ	village	قَرْيَةٌ
cars	سَيَّارَات	surah	سُورَةٌ

Learn the numbers in Arabic

Numbers

		Feminine	Masculine
one	1	وَاحِدَةٌ	وَاحِدٌ
two	2	اِثْنَتَانِ	اِثْنَانِ
three	3	ثَلَاثَةٌ	ثَلَاثٌ
four	4	أَرْبَعَةٌ	أَرْبَعٌ
five	5	خَمْسَةٌ	خَمْسٌ
six	6	سِتَّةٌ	سِتٌّ
seven	7	سَبْعَةٌ	سَبْعٌ
eight	8	ثَمَانِيَةٌ	ثَمَانٍ
nine	9	تِسْعَةٌ	تِسْعٌ
ten	10	عَشَرَةٌ	عَشْرٌ

Numbers: as with nouns and colours, numbers in Arabic also have masculine and feminine forms.

Important to note the feminine form of numbers is used when referring to masculine nouns, and the masculine form of numbers is used when referring to feminine nouns e.g.,

three books (كِتَابٌ _masculine noun_)

ثَلَاثَةُ كُتُبٍ

three cars (سَيَّارَةٌ _feminine noun_)

ثَلَاثُ سَيَّارَاتٍ

Note: the nouns will be in their plural form, and will end with two kasras

Triliteral

ذَهَبَ / يَذْهَبُ

غَسَلَ / يَغْسِلُ

كَتَبَ / يَكْتُبُ

لَعِبَ / يَلْعَبُ

UNIT 1

Triliteral with
increase letters

أَغْلَقَ / يُغْلِقُ

اِنْتَظَرَ / يَنْتَظِرُ

اِسْتَيْقَظَ / يَسْتَيْقِظُ

UNIT 2

Triliteral with
increase letters

نَظَّفَ / يُنَظِّف

تَكَلَّمَ / يَتَكَلَّمُ

سَاعَدَ / يُسَاعِدُ

UNIT 3

Assimilated

وَضَعَ / يَضَعُ

UNIT 4

Hollow

قَالَ / يَقُول

بَاعَ / يَبِيعُ

نَامَ / يَنَامُ

UNIT 5

Defective

جَرَى / يَجْرِي

نَسِيَ / يَنْسَى

دَعَا / يَدْعُو

UNIT 6

Defective

صَلَّى / يُصَلِّي

أَعْطَى / يُعْطِي

UNIT 7

Doubly week

جَاءَ / يَجِيءُ

UNIT 8

Geminate

عَدَّ / يَعُدُّ

أَحَبَّ / يُحِبُّ

UNIT 9

Hamzated

أَكَلَ / يَأْكُلُ

UNIT 10

Hollow

اِخْتَارَ / يَخْتَارُ

أَجَابَ / يُجِيبُ

UNIT 11

Study the pattern of Assimilated verbs carefully with their present and past tense together, make sure you know the meaning and verbal noun*

Assimilated Arabic Verbs

verbal noun*			present / past
putting	وَضْعٌ	put	وَضَعَ / يَضَعُ
stopping	وَقْفٌ	stand, stop	وَقَفَ / يَقِفُ
presence, existence	وُجُودٌ	find	وَجَدَ / يَجِدُ
arrival	وُصُولٌ	arrive	وَصَلَ / يَصِلُ

Read sentences, write, point on the verbs, say their past and present tense together

Sentences

وَضَعَ التِّلْمِيذُ الْكِتَابَ عَلَى الْمَكْتَبِ.

وَقَفَ مَحْمُودٌ وَرَاءَ الْبَابِ.

هُوَ وَجَدَ قَلَمِي.

وَصَلَ حَسَنٌ إِلَى الْمَطَارِ مُبَكِّرًا.

<u>To make the Imperative:</u>
- use present tense يَضَعُ يَقِفُ
- remove the present tense prefix, in this case يَ
- follow the rules of making masculine (*singular*), feminine (*singular*) and plural (*masculine*) Imperative

Study the Imperative form, used to say an order, command

Imperative verbs

masculine *singular*	Stop!	قِفْ	masculine *singular*	Put!	ضَعْ
feminine *singular*	Stop!	قِفِي	feminine *singular*	Put!	ضَعِي
plural *masculine*	Stop!	قِفُوا	plural *masculine*	Put!	ضَعُوا

*Verbal noun is a noun derived from the verb.
There is no rule for deriving the verbal noun from this pattern

Study the New words

Nouns		
airport	مَطَارٌ
train station	مَحَطَّةُ الْقِطَارِ
bus station	مَحَطَّةُ الْحَافِلَةِ
shop	مَتْجَرٌ

Study the Grammar lesson

Occupations	female	male
teacher	مُعَلِّمَةٌ	مُعَلِّمٌ
doctor	طَبِيبَةٌ	طَبِيبٌ
policeman (woman)	شُرْطِيَّةٌ	شُرْطِيٌّ
engineer	مُهَنْدِسَةٌ	مُهَنْدِسٌ
student	طَالِبَةٌ	طَالِبٌ
friend	صَدِيقَةٌ	صَدِيقٌ
child	طِفْلَةٌ	طِفْلٌ
pupil	تِلْمِيذَةٌ	تِلْمِيذٌ
grandfather (mother)	جَدَّةٌ	جَدٌّ

Remember: nouns are made feminine by adding taa marbuta ة at the end. The last letter before ة takes fatha e.g.,

مُعَلِّمٌ is male teacher

مُعَلِّمَةٌ is female teacher

Study the pattern of Hollow verbs carefully with their present and past tense together, make sure you know the meaning and verbal noun*

Hollow Arabic Verbs			present / past
verbal noun*			
saying	قَوْلٌ	say	قَالَ / يَقُولُ
visiting	زِيَارَةٌ	visit	زَارَ / يَزُورُ
returning	عَوْدَةٌ	return	عَادَ / يَعُودُ

Read sentences, write, point on the verbs, say their past and present tense together

Sentences
قَالَ سَعِيدٌ: لِي أَخٌ وَثَلاَثَةُ أَخَوَاتٍ.
زَارَ خَالِدٌ عَمَّهُ.
عَادَ سَمِيرٌ مِنَ الْمَدْرَسَةِ.
مَاذَا قَالَ أَحْمَد؟ قَالَ: عِنْدِي سَيَّارَةٌ.
لَدَيَّ أُسْرَةٌ كَبِيرَةٌ.
لَهَا أُخْتٌ. اِسْمُهَا نَادِيَة.

Study the Imperative form, used to say an order, command

Imperative verbs		
masculine *singular*	Say!	قُلْ
feminine *singular*	Say!	قُولِي
plural *masculine*	Say!	قُولُوا

<u>To make the Imperative:</u>
- use present tense يَقُولُ
- remove the present tense prefix, in this case يَ
- follow the rules of making masculine (singular), feminine (singular) and plural (masculine) Imperative

<u>Remember:</u> the letter و is omitted in masculine *singular* form

*Verbal noun is a noun derived from the verb.
There is no rule for deriving the verbal noun from this pattern

Study the New words

Nouns

uncle (dad's brother)	عَمٌّ	family	أُسْرَةٌ
uncle (mom's brother)	خَالٌ	brother	أَخٌ
son	اِبْنٌ	brothers	إِخْوَة
daughter	اِبْنَةٌ	sister	أُخْتٌ
mouth	فَمٌ	sisters	أَخَوَات

Study the Grammar lesson

Have, has

عِنْدَ	لَدَى	لِ	
عِنْدِي	لَدَيَّ	لِي	I have
عِنْدَكَ	لَدَيْكَ	لَكَ	you have (speak with male)
عِنْدَكِ	لَدَيْكِ	لَكِ	you have (speak with female)
عِنْدَهُ	لَدَيْهِ	لَهُ	he has
عِنْدَهَا	لَدَيْهَا	لَهَا	she has

To have: to say "have" in Arabic we use prepositions

عِنْدَ   لَدَى   لِ

and add possessive suffixes e.g.,

I have (عِنْدَ + ي) = عِنْدِي

He has (عِنْدَ + هُ) = عِنْدَهُ

To have: with humans and parts of body use لِ e.g.,

لِي أَخٌ

لِي فَمٌّ

Study the pattern of Hollow verbs carefully with their present and past tense together, make sure you know the meaning and verbal noun*

Hollow Arabic Verbs

verbal noun*			present / past
selling	بَيْعٌ	sell	بَاعَ / يَبِيعُ
flying, airline	طَيَرَانٌ	fly	طَارَ / يَطِيرُ
living	عِيشَةٌ	live	عَاشَ / يَعِيشُ

Read sentences, write, point on the verbs, say their past and present tense together

Sentences

يَبِيعُ عَمِّي فَوَاكِهَ فِي السُّوقِ.
طَارَ عُصْفُورٌ أَمَامَ النَّافِذَةِ.
يَعِيشُ أَخِي فِي الْقَرْيَةِ.
يَبِيعُ مُنِيرٌ بَيْتَهُ.
أَلَكِ أُخْتٌ؟ نَعَم، لِي أُخْتٌ وَاحِدَةٌ.
هَلْ عِنْدَكَ دَرَّاجَةٌ يَا أَخِي؟ نَعَم، عِنْدِي دَرَّاجَةٌ.

Study the Imperative form, used to say an order, command

Imperative verbs

masculine singular	Sell!	بِعْ
feminine singular	Sell!	بِيعِي
plural masculine	Sell!	بِيعُوا

To make the Imperative:
- use present tense يَبِيعُ
- remove the present tense prefix, in this case يَ
- follow the rules of making masculine (singular), feminine (singular) and plural (masculine) Imperative

Remember: the letter ي is omitted in masculine singular form

*Verbal noun is a noun derived from the verb.
There is no rule for deriving the verbal noun from this pattern

Study the New words

Nouns

grapes	عِنَب	market	سُوقٌ
bird	عُصْفُورٌ	fruits	فَوَاكِه
apples	تُفَّاح	fruit	فَاكِهَةٌ
oranges	بُرتُقَال	strawberries	فَرَاوِلَة

Study the Grammar lesson

Do (does) + have?

هَلْ or أَ

هَلْ عِنْدِي	هَلْ لَدَيَّ	هَلْ لِي	Do I have?
هَلْ عِنْدَكَ	هَلْ لَدَيْكَ	هَلْ لَكَ	Do you have? (speak with male)
هَلْ عِنْدِكِ	هَلْ لَدَيْكِ	هَلْ لَكِ	Do you have? (speak with female)
هَلْ عِنْدَهُ	هَلْ لَدَيْهُ	هَلْ لَهُ	Does he have?
هَلْ عِنْدَهَا	هَلْ لَدَيْهَا	هَلْ لَهَا	Does she have?

Asking questions: In Arabic questions are made by writing أَ or هَلْ in the beginning of a sentence e.g.,

Do you have a pen?

هَلْ لَدَيْكَ قَلَمٌ؟
أَلَدَيْكَ قَلَمٌ؟

Note: أَ becomes part of the following word, but هَلْ is written separately

Remember: words "yes" and "no"
Yes = نَعَم
No = لا

Study the pattern of Hollow verbs carefully with their present and past tense together, make sure you know the meaning and verbal noun*

Hollow Arabic Verbs			
verbal noun*			present / past
sleeping	نَوْمٌ	sleep	نَامَ / يَنَامُ
fear	خَوْفٌ	be afraid of	خَافَ / يَخَافُ
getting	نَيْلٌ	receive, get	نَالَ / يَنَالُ

Read sentences, write, point on the verbs, say their past and present tense together

Sentences
نَامَ الْوَلَدُ عَلَى السَّرِيرِ.
خَافَ الْفِيلُ مِنَ الْفَأْرِ.
نَالَ تِلْمِيذٌ جَائِزَةً.
يَنَامُ الْأَطْفَالُ مُبَكِّرًا.
هَلْ لَكِ أُخْتٌ؟ لَا، لَيْسَ لِي أُخْتٌ.
هَلْ عِنْدَكَ كُرَةٌ؟ نَعَم، عِنْدِي كُرَةٌ.

Study the Imperative form, used to say an order, command

Imperative verbs		
masculine *singular*	Sleep!	نَمْ
feminine *singular*	Sleep!	نَامِي
plural *masculine*	Sleep!	نَامُوا

To make the Imperative:

- use present tense يَنَامُ
- remove the present tense prefix, in this case يَ
- follow the rules of making masculine (singular), feminine (singular) and plural (masculine) Imperative

Remember: the letter ا is omitted in masculine singular form

*Verbal noun is a noun derived from the verb.
There is no rule for deriving the verbal noun from this pattern

Study the New words

Nouns

mouse	فَأْرٌ	prize	جَائِزَةٌ
elephant	فِيلٌ	animal	حَيَوَان
bed	سَرِيرٌ	rabbit	أَرْنَبٌ
children	أَطْفَال	lion	أَسَدٌ

Study the Grammar lesson

Don't have, doesn't have

لَيْسَ

لَيْسَ عِنْدِي	لَيْسَ لَدَيَّ	لَيْسَ لِي	I don't have
لَيْسَ عِنْدَكَ	لَيْسَ لَدَيْكَ	لَيْسَ لَكَ	you don't have (speak with male)
لَيْسَ عِنْدَكِ	لَيْسَ لَدَيْكِ	لَيْسَ لَكِ	you don't have (speak with female)
لَيْسَ عِنْدَهُ	لَيْسَ لَدَيْهِ	لَيْسَ لَهُ	he doesn't have
لَيْسَ عِنْدَهَا	لَيْسَ لَدَيْهَا	لَيْسَ لَهَا	she doesn't have

Don't have, doesn't have: to say "don't have" or "doesn't have" in Arabic we use negative particle لَيْسَ

I don't have a car
لَيْسَ عِنْدِي سَيَّارَةٌ

He doesn't have a car
لَيْسَ عِنْدَهُ سَيَّارَةٌ

Remember: with humans and parts of body use لِ e.g., I don't have brother
لَيْسَ لِي أَخٌ

Triliteral

ذَهَبَ / يَذْهَبُ
غَسَلَ / يَغْسِلُ
كَتَبَ / يَكْتُبُ
لَعِبَ / يَلْعَبُ

UNIT 1

Triliteral with increase letters

أَغْلَقَ / يُغْلِقُ
اِنْتَظَرَ / يَنْتَظِرُ
اِسْتَيْقَظَ / يَسْتَيْقِظُ

UNIT 2

Triliteral with increase letters

نَظَّفَ / يُنَظِّف
تَكَلَّمَ / يَتَكَلَّمُ
سَاعَدَ / يُسَاعِدُ

UNIT 3

Assimilated

وَضَعَ / يَضَعُ

UNIT 4

Hollow

قَالَ / يَقُول
بَاعَ / يَبِيعُ
نَامَ / يَنَامُ

UNIT 5

Defective

جَرَى / يَجْرِي
نَسِيَ / يَنْسَى
دَعَا / يَدْعُو

UNIT 6

Defective

صَلَّى / يُصَلِّي
أَعْطَى / يُعْطِي

UNIT 7

Doubly week

جَاءَ / يَجِيءُ

UNIT 8

Geminate

عَدَّ / يَعُدُّ
أَحَبَّ / يُحِبُّ

UNIT 9

Hamzated

أَكَلَ / يَأْكُلُ

UNIT 10

Hollow

اِخْتَارَ / يَخْتَارُ
أَجَابَ / يُجِيبُ

UNIT 11

Study the pattern of Defective verbs carefully with their present and past tense together, make sure you know the meaning and verbal noun*

Defective Arabic Verbs

verbal noun*			present / past
running	جَرْيٌ	run	جَرَى / يَجْرِي
crying	بُكَاءٌ	cry	بَكَى / يَبْكِي
building	بِنَاءٌ	build	بَنَى / يَبْنِي
buying	اِشْتِرَاءٌ	buy	اِشْتَرَى / يَشْتَرِي
wearing	اِرْتِدَاءٌ	wear	اِرْتَدَى / يَرْتَدِي
meeting	اِلْتِقَاءٌ	meet	اِلْتَقَى / يَلْتَقِي

To make the Imperative:

- use present tense يَجْرِي
- remove the present tense prefix, in this case يَ and replace it with alif ا with kasrah اِ
- follow the rules of making masculine (singular), feminine (singular) and plural (masculine) Imperative

Study the Imperative form, used to say an order, command

Imperative verbs

masculine singular	Run!	اِجْرِ
feminine singular	Run!	اِجْرِي
plural masculine	Run!	اِجْرُوا

Read sentences, write, point on the verbs, say their past and present tense together

Sentences

هُوَ جَرَى إِلَى بَيْتِهِ.
يَبْكِي أَخِي كَثِيرًا.
بَنَى جَمَالٌ قَصْرًا.

هُوَ اِشْتَرَى قَلَمًا مِنَ السُّوقِ.
هُوَ اِرْتَدَى مَلَابِسَهُ.
اِلْتَقَى أَحْمَدُ بِصَدِيقِهِ فِي الْمَدِينَةِ.

Remember: : in masculine *singular* form last letter takes kasrah not sukuun

*Verbal noun is a noun derived from the verb.
There is no rule for deriving the verbal nouns for following verbs of pattern جَرَى / يَجْرِي
For pattern اِشْتَرَى / يَشْتَرِي verbal noun are made by following pattern اِفْتِعَالٌ

34

Study the New words

Nouns			
morning	صَبَاحٌ	house	مَنْزِلٌ
evening	مَسَاءٌ	castle	قَصْرٌ
time	وَقْتٌ	notebook	دَفْتَرٌ

Study the Grammar lesson

Had / didn't have

كَانَ / مَا كَانَ

كَانَ/ مَا كَانَ عِنْدِي	كَانَ/ مَا كَانَ لَدَيَّ	كَانَ/ مَا كَانَ لِي	I had / didn't have
كَانَ/ مَا كَانَ عِنْدَكَ	كَانَ/ مَا كَانَ لَدَيْكَ	كَانَ/ مَا كَانَ لَكَ	you had / didn't have (speak with male)
كَانَ/ مَا كَانَ عِنْدَكِ	كَانَ/ مَا كَانَ لَدَيْكِ	كَانَ/ مَا كَانَ لَكِ	you had / didn't have (speak with female)
كَانَ/ مَا كَانَ عِنْدَهُ	كَانَ/ مَا كَانَ لَدَيْهُ	كَانَ/ مَا كَانَ لَهُ	he had / didn't have
كَانَ/ مَا كَانَ عِنْدَهَا	كَانَ/ مَا كَانَ لَدَيْهَا	كَانَ/ مَا كَانَ لَهَا	she had / didn't have

Study the prepositions and question words

Prepositions		
هُوَ اِشْتَرَى دَفْتَرًا لِصَدِيقِهِ.	to, for, belongs to	لِ
He bought notebook for his friend		
هَذَا الْقَلَمُ لِحَامِدٍ.	to, for, belongs to	لِ
This pen belongs to Hamid		

Had, didn't have:

• to say "had" in Arabic we use past tense verb كَانَ which means "was"

I had a car
كَانَ عِنْدِي سَيَّارَةٌ.

• to say "didn't have" in Arabic we use past tense verb مَا + كَانَ

I didn't have time
مَا كَانَ عِنْدِي وَقْتٌ.

Study the pattern of Defective verbs carefully with their present and past tense together, make sure you know the meaning and verbal noun*

Defective Arabic Verbs

verbal noun*				present / past
forgetfulness	نِسْيَانٌ		forget	نَسِيَ / يَنْسَى
remaining	بَقَاءٌ		stay, remain	بَقِيَ / يَبْقَى

Read sentences, write, point on the verbs, say their past and present tense together

Sentences

نَسِيَ حَسَنٌ مِظَلَّتَهُ.

بَقِيَ الْوَلَدُ فِي الْمَنْزِلِ.

نَسِيَ عَلِيٌّ كُرَتَهُ.

يَبْقَى بِلَالٌ فِي قَرْيَتِهِ.

هُوَ يَرْتَدِي مَلَابِسَ الصَّيْفِ.

يَنَامُ الدُّبُّ فِي فَصْلِ الشِّتَاءِ.

Study the Imperative form, used to say an order, command

Imperative verbs

masculine *singular*	Forget!	اِنْسَ
feminine *singular*	Forget!	اِنْسِي
plural *masculine*	Forget!	اِنْسَوْا

To make the Imperative:

- use present tense يَنْسَى
- remove the present tense prefix, in this case يَ and replace it with alif ا with kasrah اِ
- for masculine (singular) remove the last letter ى
- for feminine (singular) replace ى with ي
- for plural (masculine) replace ى with وْ

*Verbal noun is a noun derived from the verb.
There is no rule for deriving the verbal noun from this pattern

Study the New words

Nouns

moon	قَمَرٌ	umbrella	مِظَلَّةٌ
sea	بَحْرٌ	rain	مَطَرٌ
river	نَهْرٌ	sun	شَمْسٌ

Learn the seasons of the year

Seasons

spring	فَصْلُ الرَّبِيع
summer	فَصْلُ الصَّيْف
autumn	فَصْلُ الْخَرِيف
winter	فَصْلُ الشِّتَاء

Learn the names of animals

Animals

dog	كَلْبٌ	cow	بَقَرَةٌ
cat	قِطَّةٌ	monkey	قِرْدٌ
horse	حِصَانٌ	bear	دُبٌّ
donkey	حِمَارٌ	bee	نَحْلَةٌ
ant	نَمْلَةٌ	fox	ثَعْلَبٌ
camel	جَمَلٌ	chicken	دَجَاجَةٌ

Triliteral	
ذَهَبَ / يَذْهَبُ	
غَسَلَ / يَغْسِلُ	UNIT 1
كَتَبَ / يَكْتُبُ	
لَعِبَ / يَلْعَبُ	
Triliteral with increase letters	
أَغْلَقَ / يُغْلِقُ	
إِنْتَظَرَ / يَنْتَظِرُ	UNIT 2
إِسْتَيْقَظَ / يَسْتَيْقِظُ	
Triliteral with increase letters	
نَظَّفَ / يُنَظِّف	
تَكَلَّمَ / يَتَكَلَّمُ	UNIT 3
سَاعَدَ / يُسَاعِدُ	
Assimilated	
وَضَعَ / يَضَعُ	UNIT 4
Hollow	
قَالَ / يَقُول	
بَاعَ / يَبِيعُ	UNIT 5
نَامَ / يَنَامُ	
Defective	
جَرَى / يَجْرِي	
نَسِيَ / يَنْسَى	UNIT 6
دَعَا / يَدْعُو	
Defective	
صَلَّى / يُصَلِّي	UNIT 7
أَعْطَى / يُعْطِي	
Doubly week	
جَاءَ / يَجِيءُ	UNIT 8
Geminate	
عَدَّ / يَعُدُّ	UNIT 9
أَحَبَّ / يُحِبُّ	
Hamzated	
أَكَلَ / يَأْكُلُ	UNIT 10
Hollow	
إِخْتَارَ / يَخْتَارُ	UNIT 11
أَجَابَ / يُجِيبُ	

Study the pattern of Defective verbs carefully with their present and past tense together, make sure you know the meaning and verbal noun*

Defective Arabic Verbs				present / past
verbal noun*				present / past
call, invitation	دَعْوَةٌ	call, invite		دَعَا / يَدْعُو
reciting	تُلُوٌّ	recite, follow		تَلَا / يَتْلُو

Read sentences, write, point on the verbs, say their past and present tense together

Sentences
دَعَا مُحَمَّدٌ إِلَى الله.
تَلَا الْإِمَامُ سُورَةَ الْفِيل.
دَعَا سَلِيمٌ صَدِيقَهُ إِلَى بَيْتِه.
يَتْلُو عَبْدُ اللهِ سُورَةَ الرَّحْمَان.
بِنْتٌ صَغِيرَةٌ.
صُورَةٌ جَمِيلَةٌ.
مُعَلِّمٌ جَيِّدٌ.

Study the Imperative form, used to say an order, command

Imperative verbs		
masculine *singular*	Call, invite!	أُدْعُ
feminine *singular*	Call, invite!	أُدْعِي
plural *masculine*	Call, invite!	أُدْعُوا

<u>To make the Imperative:</u>

- use present tense يَدْعُو
- remove the present tense prefix, in this case يَ and replace it with alif ا with damma أُ
- follow the rules of making masculine *(singular)*, feminine *(singular)* and plural *(masculine)* Imperative

Remember: : in masculine *singular* form last letter takes damma not sukuun

*Verbal noun is a noun derived from the verb.
There is no rule for deriving the verbal noun from this pattern

Study the New words

Nouns			
Imam, leader of prayer	إِمَامٌ	surah	سُورَةٌ
voice	صَوْتٌ	picture	صُورَةٌ
forest	غَابَةٌ	guest	ضَيْفٌ

Study the Grammar lesson

Adjectives		
	feminine	masculine
big	كَبِيرَةٌ	كَبِيرٌ
small	صَغِيرَةٌ	صَغِيرٌ
beautiful	جَمِيلَةٌ	جَمِيلٌ
new	جَدِيدَةٌ	جَدِيدٌ
old	قَدِيمَةٌ	قَدِيمٌ
good	جَيِّدَةٌ	جَيِّدٌ

Adjectives: In Arabic adjectives (describing words) come after the nouns.

When the noun is masculine, the adjective also will be masculine e.g.,

a big house

بَيْتٌ كَبِيرٌ.

When the noun is feminine, the adjective will also be feminine

a beautiful park

حَدِيقَةٌ جَمِيلَةٌ.

Triliteral	UNIT 1

ذَهَبَ / يَذْهَبُ
غَسَلَ / يَغْسِلُ
كَتَبَ / يَكْتُبُ
لَعِبَ / يَلْعَبُ

Triliteral with increase letters — UNIT 2

أَغْلَقَ / يُغْلِقُ
اِنْتَظَرَ / يَنْتَظِرُ
اِسْتَيْقَظَ / يَسْتَيْقِظُ

Triliteral with increase letters — UNIT 3

نَظَّفَ / يُنَظِّفُ
تَكَلَّمَ / يَتَكَلَّمُ
سَاعَدَ / يُسَاعِدُ

Assimilated — UNIT 4

وَضَعَ / يَضَعُ

Hollow — UNIT 5

قَالَ / يَقُولُ
بَاعَ / يَبِيعُ
نَامَ / يَنَامُ

Defective — UNIT 6

جَرَى / يَجْرِي
نَسِيَ / يَنْسَى
دَعَا / يَدْعُو

Defective — UNIT 7

صَلَّى / يُصَلِّي
أَعْطَى / يُعْطِي

Doubly week — UNIT 8

جَاءَ / يَجِيءُ

Geminate — UNIT 9

عَدَّ / يَعُدُّ
أَحَبَّ / يُحِبُّ

Hamzated — UNIT 10

أَكَلَ / يَأْكُلُ

Hollow — UNIT 11

اِخْتَارَ / يَخْتَارُ
أَجَابَ / يُجِيبُ

Study the pattern of Defective verbs carefully with their present and past tense together, make sure you know the meaning and verbal noun*

Defective Arabic Verbs

verbal noun*			present / past
prayer	صَلَاةٌ	pray	صَلَّى / يُصَلِّي
naming	تَسْمِيَةٌ	name	سَمَّى / يُسَمِّي

Read sentences, write, point on the verbs, say their past and present tense together

Sentences

صَلَّى بَشِيرٌ فِي الْمَسْجِدِ.

سَمَّى بِلَالٌ اِبْنَهُ أَحْمَدًا.

يُصَلِّي الْمُسْلِمُ خَمْسَ صَلَوَاتٍ كُلَّ يَوْمٍ.

هُوَ يُصَلِّي صلاةَ الْعَصْرِ فِي الْمَسْجِدِ.

سَمَّى الْأَبُ اِبْنَتَهُ عَائِشَةَ.

فَتَحَ طَارِقٌ الصُّنْدُوقَ الْكَبِيرَ.

Study the Imperative form, used to say an order, command

Imperative verbs

masculine singular	Pray!	صَلِّ
feminine singular	Pray!	صَلِّي
plural masculine	Pray!	صَلُّوا

<u>To make the Imperative:</u>

- use present tense يُصَلِّي
- remove the present tense prefix, in this case يُ
- follow the rules of making masculine (singular), feminine (singular) and plural (masculine) Imperative

<u>*Remember:*</u> : in masculine *singular* form last letter takes kasrah not sukuun

*Verbal noun is a noun derived from the verb.
There is no rule for deriving the verbal noun from this pattern

Study the New words

Nouns

mosque	مَسْجِدٌ	Fajr prayer	صَلَاةُ الفَجْرِ
prayer	صَلَاةٌ	Dhuhr prayer	صَلَاةُ الظُّهْرِ
prayers	صَلَوَات	Asr prayer	صَلَاةُ العَصْرِ
every day	كُلَّ يَوْمٍ	Maghrib prayer	صَلَاةُ المَغْرِبِ
		Isha prayer	صَلَاةُ العِشَاءِ

Study the Grammar lesson

Adjective + Noun (indefinite)	Adjective + Noun (definite)
صُنْدُوقٌ كَبِيرٌ	الصُّنْدُوقُ الْكَبِيرُ
a big box	the big box
شَجَرَةٌ صَغِيرَةٌ	الشَّجَرَةُ الصَّغِيرَةُ
a small tree	the small tree
حَدِيقَةٌ جَمِيلَةٌ	الْحَدِيقَةُ الْجَمِيلَةُ
a beautiful park	the beautiful park
مَكْتَبٌ جَدِيدٌ	الْمَكْتَبُ الْجَدِيدُ
a new desk	the new desk
بَيْتٌ قَدِيمٌ	الْبَيْتُ الْقَدِيمُ
an old house	the old house
مُعَلِّمَةٌ جَيِّدَةٌ	الْمُعَلِّمَةُ الْجَيِّدَةُ
a good teacher (female)	the good teacher (female)

Remember: if the noun is definite the adjective is also definite.

And if the noun is indefinite so the adjective is also indefinite

*Study the pattern of Defective verbs carefully with their present and past tense together, make sure you know the meaning and verbal noun**

Defective Arabic Verbs

verbal noun*			present / past
giving	إِعْطَاءٌ	give	أَعْطَى / يُعْطِي
throwing	إِلْقَاءٌ	throw	أَلْقَى / يُلْقِي

Read sentences, write, point on the verbs, say their past and present tense together

Sentences

أَعْطَى سَمِيرٌ كِتَابًا لِصَدِيقِهِ.

أَلْقَى صَالِحٌ سَمَكَةً فِي الْمَاءِ.

هُوَ أَعْطَى الْكِتَابَ لِلْمُعَلِّمَةِ.

أَلْقَى طَارِقٌ كُرَةً فِي السَّلَّةِ.

أَعْطِنِي كُوبًا مِنَ الشَّايِ.

أَعْطِينِي كَأْسَ الْمَاءِ.

To make the Imperative:

- use present tense يُعْطِي
- remove the present tense prefix, in this case يُ and replace it with alif ا with fatha أَ
- follow the rules of making masculine (singular), feminine (singular) and plural (masculine) Imperative

Remember: in masculine singular form last letter takes kasrah not sukuun

Study the Imperative form, used to say an order, command

Imperative verbs

masculine singular	Give!	أَعْطِ	masculine singular	Give me!	أَعْطِنِي
feminine singular	Give!	أَعْطِي	feminine singular	Give me!	أَعْطِينِي
plural masculine	Give!	أَعْطُوا	plural masculine	Give me!	أَعْطُونِي

*Verbal noun is a noun derived from the verb.
There is a rule for deriving the verbal noun from this pattern. Verbal noun are made by following pattern إِفْعَالٌ

Study the New words

Nouns

tea	شَايٌّ	sweet, candy	حَلْوَى
coffee	قَهْوَةٌ	basket	سَلَّةٌ
fish	سَمَكَةٌ	cup	كَأْسٌ
juice	عَصِيرٌ	cup	كُوبٌ

Learn parts of the body

Body parts

body	جِسْمٌ
head	رَأْسٌ
face	وَجْهٌ
eye	عَيْنٌ
nose	أَنْفٌ
ear	أُذُنٌ
mouth	فَمٌ
tongue	لِسَانٌ
lip	شَفَةٌ
hand	يَدٌ
leg	رِجْلٌ
foot	قَدَمٌ

Remember: all nouns in Arabic are either masculine of feminine.

Double members of the body are feminine while single members are masculine, e.g.

هَذَا أَنْفٌ وَهَذَا فَمٌ
هَذِهِ يَدٌ وَهَذِهِ رِجْلٌ

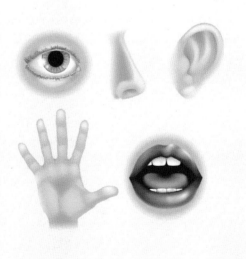

43

Study the pattern of Doubly week verbs carefully with their present and past tense together, make sure you know the meaning and verbal noun*

Doubly week Arabic Verbs

verbal noun*			present / past
coming	مَجِيءٌ	come	جَاءَ / يَجِيءُ
seeing, vision	رُؤْيَةٌ	see	رَأَى / يَرَى
coming	إِتْيَانٌ	come, arrive, bring	أَتَى / يَأْتِي

Study the Imperative form, used to say an order, command

Imperative verbs

masculine singular	See!	رَ
feminine singular	See!	رَيْ
plural masculine	See!	رَوْا
masculine singular	Come!	جِىءْ
feminine singular	Come!	جِيئِي
plural masculine	Come!	جِيئُوا
masculine singular	Come!	ائْتِ
feminine singular	Come!	ائْتِي
plural masculine	Come!	ائْتُوا

Read sentences, write, point on the verbs, say their past and present tense together

Sentences

جَاءَ الْقِطَارُ مُتَأَخِّرًا.
أَنَا أَرَى شَجَرَةً كَبِيرَةً.
يَأْتِي عِيدُ الْفِطْرِ بَعْدَ شَهْرِ رَمَضَانَ.

To make the Imperative:
- use present tense يَأْتِي
- remove the present tense prefix, in this case يَ and replace it with alif ا with kasrah اِ
- follow the rules of making masculine (singular), feminine (singular) and plural (masculine) Imperative

Remember: : in masculine singular form last letter takes kasrah not sukuun

*Verbal noun is a noun derived from the verb.
There is no rule for deriving the verbal noun from this pattern

44

Study the New words

Nouns

week	أُسْبُوعٌ	day	يَوْمٌ
year	عَامٌ	months	شَهْرٌ

Study the words related to the Religion

Religion

Religion	دِينٌ
Ramadan	رَمَضَان
Eid al-Fitr	عِيدُ الْفِطْرِ
Eid al-Adha	عِيدُ الْأَضْحَى
Messenger	رَسُولٌ
Prophet	نَبِيٌّ
Noble Makkah	مَكَّةُ الْمُكَرَّمَة

Study the Adverbs

Adverbs

يَأْتِي فَصْلُ الشِّتَاءُ بَعْدَ فَصْلِ الْخَرِيفِ. The winter comes after the autumn	after	بَعْدَ
زَارَ مُحَمَّدٌ عَمَّهُ قَبْلَ شَهْرِ رَمَضَانِ. Muhamad visited his uncle before the month of Ramadan		
هُوَ ذَهَبَ إِلَى مَكَّةِ الْمُكَرَّمَةِ قَبْلَ شَهْرِ. He went to the Noble Makkah a month ago	before, ago	قَبْلَ

Study the pattern of Geminate verbs carefully with their present and past tense together, make sure you know the meaning and verbal noun*

Geminate Arabic Verbs			
verbal noun*			present / past
counting	عَدٌّ	count	عَدَّ / يَعُدُّ
smelling	شَمٌّ	smell	شَمَّ / يَشُمُّ

Read sentences, write, point on the verbs, say their past and present tense together

Sentences
يَعُدُّ الْوَلَدُ الْأَحْجَارَ.
يَشُمُّ بِلَالٌ رَائِحَةَ الزُّهُورِ.
يَعُدُّ أَحْمَدُ الزُّهُورَ.
يَشُمُّ صَالِحٌ زَهْرَةً.
يَعُدُّ فَيْصَلٌ: وَاحِد، اِثْنَان، ثَلَاثَة، أَرْبَعَةً...
أَيْنَ كِتَابُ مُحَمَّدٍ؟ هُوَ عَلَى الْمَكْتَبِ.

Study the Imperative form, used to say an order, command

Imperative verbs		
masculine *singular*	Count!	عُدَّ
feminine *singular*	Count!	عُدِّي
plural *masculine*	Count!	عُدُّوا

To make the Imperative:

- use present tense يَعُدُّ
- remove the present tense prefix, in this case يَ
- follow the rules of making masculine (singular), feminine (singular) and plural (masculine) Imperative

Remember: : in masculine *singular* form last letter takes fatha not sukuun

*Verbal noun is a noun derived from the verb.
There is no rule for deriving the verbal noun from this pattern

Study the New words

Nouns			
smell	رَائِحَةٌ	flower	زَهْرَةٌ
mountain	جَبَلٌ	flowers	زُهُور
mountains	جِبَال	stone	حَجَرٌ
key	مِفْتَاحٌ	stones	أَحْجَار

Study the Grammar lesson

Relationship between two nouns Idaafah

the Imam's house	بَيْتُ الْإِمَامِ
the key of the car	مِفْتَاحُ السَّيَّارَةِ
son of Karim	اِبْنُ كَرِيمٍ
the messenger of Allah	رَسُولُ اللهِ
the name of the student	اِسْمُ الطَّالِبِ
the book of Allah	كِتَابُ اللهِ

Idaafah occurs when two nouns are linked together and is similar to English "of" or "s" which express belonging, e.g.
Bilal's book كِتَابُ بِلَالٍ
the teacher's book
or the book of the teacher
كِتَابُ الْمُعَلِّمِ

Remember: the mudaaf in our case كِتَابُ is definite by position and does not need the definite article. The mudaaf ilaihi in our case الْمُعَلِّم and بِلَالٍ is in the genitive case

Study the pattern of Geminate verbs carefully with their present and past tense together, make sure you know the meaning and verbal noun*

Geminate Arabic Verbs			
verbal noun*			present / past
loving, love	إِحْبَابٌ	love, like	أَحَبَّ / يُحِبُّ
preparation	إِعْدَادٌ	prepare	أَعَدَّ / يُعِدُّ

Read sentences, write, point on the verbs, say their past and present tense together

Sentences
يُحِبُّ حَسَنٌ عَائِلَتَهُ.
هُوَ يُعِدُّ الْفُطُورَ كُلَّ صَبَاح.
يُحِبُّ فَيْصَلٌ رُكُوبَ الدَّرَّاجَةِ.
يُعِدُّ بِلَالٌ الْغَدَاءَ فِي الْمَطْبِخِ.
يُحِبُّ إِبْرَاهِيمٌ تَعَلُّمَ اللُّغَةِ الْعَرَبِيَّةِ.
يَزُورُ عَبْدُ اللهِ جَدَّهُ كُلَّ يَوْمٍ.

Study the Imperative form, used to say an order, command

Imperative verbs		
masculine *singular*	Love!	أَحِبَّ
feminine *singular*	Love!	أَحِبِّي
plural *masculine*	Love!	أَحِبُّوا

To make the Imperative:

- use present tense يُحِبُّ
- remove the present tense prefix, in this case يُ and replace it with alif ا with fatha أَ
- follow the rules of making masculine *(singular)*, feminine *(singular)* and plural *(masculine)* Imperative

Remember: : in masculine *singular* form last letter takes fatha not sukuun

*Verbal noun is a noun derived from the verb.
There is a rule for deriving the verbal noun from this pattern. Verbal noun are made by following pattern إِحْبَابٌ

Study the New words

Nouns

supper	عَشَاءٌ	family	عَائِلَةٌ
breakfast	فُطُورٌ	food	طَعَامٌ
table	مَائِدَةٌ	kitchen	مَطْبَخٌ
		lunch	غَدَاءٌ

Study the Grammar lesson

Every

كُلّ

يُنَظِّفُ طَارِقٌ أَسْنَانَهُ كُلَّ صَبَاحٍ.	every morning	كُلَّ صَبَاحٍ
يَشْرَبُ مُنِيرٌ حَلِيبًا كُلَّ مَسَاءٍ.	every evening	كُلَّ مَسَاءٍ
يَذْهَبُ أَبِي إِلَى السُّوقِ كُلَّ يَوْمٍ.	every day	كُلَّ يَوْمٍ
يَلْعَبُ بِلَالٌ كُرَةَ الْقَدَمِ كُلَّ أُسْبُوعٍ.	every week	كُلَّ أُسْبُوعٍ

Study the prepositions

Prepositions

جَلَسَتِ الْعَائِلَةُ حَوْلَ الْمَائِدَةِ.	around	حَوْلَ

The family sat around the table

Triliteral	UNIT 1
ذَهَبَ / يَذْهَبُ	
غَسَلَ / يَغْسِلُ	
كَتَبَ / يَكْتُبُ	
لِعِبَ / يَلْعَبُ	

Triliteral with increase letters	UNIT 2
أَغْلَقَ / يُغْلِقُ	
إِنْتَظَرَ / يَنْتَظِرُ	
إِسْتَيْقَظَ / يَسْتَيْقِظُ	

Triliteral with increase letters	UNIT 3
نَظَّفَ / يُنَظِّفُ	
تَكَلَّمَ / يَتَكَلَّمُ	
سَاعَدَ / يُسَاعِدُ	

Assimilated	UNIT 4
وَضَعَ / يَضَعُ	

Hollow	UNIT 5
قَالَ / يَقُول	
بَاعَ / يَبِيعُ	
نَامَ / يَنَامُ	

Defective	UNIT 6
جَرَى / يَجْرِي	
نَسِيَ / يَنْسَى	
دَعَا / يَدْعُو	

Defective	UNIT 7
صَلَّى / يُصَلِّي	
أَعْطَى / يُعْطِي	

Doubly week	UNIT 8
جَاءَ / يَجِيءُ	

Geminate	UNIT 9
عَدَّ / يَعُدُّ	
أَحَبَّ / يُحِبُّ	

Hamzated	UNIT 10
أَكَلَ / يَأْكُلُ	

Hollow	UNIT 11
إِخْتَارَ / يَخْتَارُ	
أَجَابَ / يُجِيبُ	

Study the pattern of Hamzated verbs carefully with their present and past tense together, make sure you know the meaning and verbal noun*

Hamzated Arabic Verbs

verbal noun*			present / past
			hamza in the beginning
food, eating	أَكْلٌ	eat	أَكَلَ / يَأْكُلُ
taking	أَخْذٌ	take	أَخَذَ / يَأْخُذُ
			hamza in the end
reading	قِرَاءَةٌ	read	قَرَأَ / يَقْرَأُ
			hamza in the middle
question, asking	سُؤَالٌ	ask	سَأَلَ / يَسْأَلُ

Study the Imperative form, used to say an order, command

Imperative verbs

masculine *singular*	Eat!	كُلْ
feminine *singular*	Eat!	كُلِي
plural *masculine*	Eat!	كُلُوا
masculine *singular*	Read!	اِقْرَأْ
feminine *singular*	Read!	اِقْرَئِي
plural *masculine*	Read!	اِقْرَأُوا
masculine *singular*	Read!	اِسْأَلْ
feminine *singular*	Read!	اِسْأَلِي
plural *masculine*	Read!	اِسْأَلُوا

Read sentences, write, point on the verbs, say their past and present tense together

Sentences

أَكَلَ هِشَامٌ فِي الْمَطْعَمِ.

أَخَذَ الْمُعَلِّمُ الْكُرَّاسَةَ مِنَ الْوَلَدِ.

يَقْرَأُ بِلَالٌ كِتَابًا.

سَأَلَ الْمُعَلِّمُ السُّؤَالَ.

<u>To make the Imperative:</u>

- use present tense يَأْكُلُ
- remove the present tense prefix, in this case يَ and hamza with sukun أْ
- follow the rules of making masculine (*singular*), feminine (*singular*) and plural (*masculine*) Imperative

*Verbal noun is a noun derived from the verb.
There is no rule for deriving the verbal noun from this pattern

Study the New words

Nouns

question	سُؤَالٌ	
food	أَكْلٌ	
bread	خُبْزٌ	
restaurant	مَطْعَمٌ	

Study the Grammar lesson

Adverbs

أَيْنَ هُوَ الْآنَ؟	now	الآن
أَكَلَ حَسَنٌ فِي الْمَطْعَمِ الْبَارِحَةِ.	last night	الْبَارِحَة
ذَهَبَ أَبِي إِلَى السُّوقِ فِي الْأَمْسِ.	yesterday	أَمْس
هُوَ سَيَلْعَبُ كُرَةَ الْقَدَمِ غَدًا.	tomorrow	غَدًا

Study the Adverbs

Adjectives

هَذَا كَبِيرٌ جِدًّا. this is very big	very	جِدًّا
هَذَا أَيْضًا جَمِيلٌ. this is also beautiful	also, as well, too	أَيْضًا

Study the pattern of Hollow verbs carefully with their present and past tense together, make sure you know the meaning and verbal noun*

Hollow Arabic Verbs

verbal noun*			present / past
choosing, choice	اِخْتِيَارٌ	choose	اِخْتَارَ / يَخْتَارُ
need	اِحْتِيَاجٌ	need	اِحْتَاجَ / يَحْتَاجُ
hunting	اِصْطِيَادٌ	hunt	اِصْطَادَ / يَصْطَادُ

Read sentences, write, point on the verbs, say their past and present tense together

Sentences

يَخْتَارُ بَشِيرٌ اللُّعْبَةَ ثُمَّ يَلْعَبُ بِهَا.

يَحْتَاجُ كَرِيمٌ إِلَى مِسْطَرَةٍ.

يَصْطَادُ صَالِحٌ الطُّيُورَ.

اِخْتَارَ الطِّفْلُ الْحَلْوَى.

يَصْطَادُ طَارِقٌ فَرَاشَةً.

هُوَ يَحْتَاجُ إِلِي الْمَاءِ.

Study the Imperative form, used to say an order, command

Imperative verbs

masculine *singular*	Choose!	اِخْتَرْ
feminine *singular*	Choose!	اِخْتَارِي
plural *masculine*	Choose!	اِخْتَارُوا

<u>To make the Imperative:</u>

• use present tense يَخْتَارُ
• remove the present tense prefix, in this case يَ and replace it with alif ا with kasrah اِ
• follow the rules of making masculine (*singular*), feminine (*singular*) and plural (*masculine*) Imperative

<u>Remember:</u> the letter ا is omitted in masculine *singular* form

*Verbal noun is a noun derived from the verb.
There is a rule for deriving the verbal noun from this pattern. Verbal noun are made by following pattern اِحْتِيَاج

Study the New words

Nouns

time	وَقْتٌ	butterfly	فَرَاشَةٌ
ruler	مِسْطَرَةٌ	doll	دُمْيَةٌ
night	لَيْلٌ	bird	طَيْرٌ
		birds	طُيُورٌ

Study the Grammar lesson

Nominal sentence

the box is big	الصُّنْدُوقُ ـ كَبِيرٌ
the tree is small	الشَّجَرَةُ ـ صَغِيرَةٌ
the park is beautiful	الْحَدِيقَةُ ـ جَمِيلَةٌ
the desk is new	الْمَكْتَبُ ـ جَدِيدٌ
the house is old	الْبَيْتُ ـ قَدِيمٌ
the teacher (female) is good	الْمُعَلِّمَةُ ـ جَيِّدَةٌ

Nominal sentence: There are two types of Arabic sentences: nominal sentences and verbal sentences.

A _nominal sentence_ doesn't contain a verb and consists of subject and predicate.

Subject is at the beginning of sentence and is **definite**

Predicate gives information about subject and is **indefinite**

Note: a nominal sentence refers to the present tense and does not require verb "to be"

Study the pattern of Hollow verbs carefully with their present and past tense together, make sure you know the meaning and verbal noun*

Hollow Arabic Verbs			
verbal noun*			present / past
answering, answer	إِجَابَةٌ	answer	أَجَابَ / يُجِيبُ
wanting, will	إِرَادَةٌ	want	أَرَادَ / يُرِيدُ
obeying, obedience	إِطَاعَةٌ	obey	أَطَاعَ / يَطِيعُ

Read sentences, write, point on the verbs, say their past and present tense together

Sentences
أَرَادَ أَحْمَدُ أَنْ يَشْتَرِيَ الْكِتَابَ.
يُجِيبُ وَلَدٌ مُعَلِّمَتَهُ.
الْمُسْلِمُ يُطِيعُ اللَّهَ.
يُجِيبُ حَسَنٌ عَلَى السُّؤَالِ.
يُرِيدُ بِلَالٌ الذَّهَابَ إِلَى السُّوقِ.
أَنَا أُطِيعُ وَالِدَيَّ.

Study the Imperative form, used to say an order, command

Imperative verbs		
masculine *singular*	Answer!	أَجِبْ
feminine *singular*	Answer!	أَجِيبِي
plural *masculine*	Answer!	أَجِيبُوا

To make the Imperative:

- use present tense يُجِيبُ
- remove the present tense prefix, in this case يُ and replace it with alif ا with fatha أَ
- follow the rules of making masculine (*singular*), feminine (*singular*) and plural (*masculine*) Imperative

Remember: the letter ي is omitted in masculine *singular* form

*Verbal noun is a noun derived from the verb.
There is a rule for deriving the verbal noun from this pattern. Verbal noun are made by following pattern إِرَادَةٌ

Study the New words

Nouns			
parents (two)	وَالِدَيْن	answer	إِجَابَةٌ
people	نَاس	watch	سَاعَةٌ
children	أَوْلَاد	parent (father)	وَالِدٌ
		parent (mother)	وَالِدَةٌ

Study the days of the week

Days of the week	
Sunday	يَوْمُ الْأَحَد
Monday	يَوْمُ الْإِثْنَيْن
Tuesday	يَوْمُ الثُّلَاثَاء
Wednesday	يومُ الْأَرْبِعَاء
Thursday	يومُ الْخَمِيس
Friday	يومُ الْجُمُعَة
Saturday	يومُ السَّبْت

Sunday
Monday
Tuesday
Wednesday
Thursday
Friday
Saturday

Write Imperative verbs

masculine *singular*	Do!	....	masculine *singular*	Open!	....
feminine *singular*	Do!	....	feminine *singular*	Open!	....
plural *masculine*	Do!	....	plural *masculine*	Open!	....

Write in the missing words

مَاذَا	فَتَحَ الْوَلَدُ ....
بِنْتٌ	.... أَحْمَدُ إِلَى الْمَلْعَبِ.
فَتَحَ	.... يَفْعَلُ سَعِيد؟
أَحْمَدُ	ذَهَبَ سَمِيرٌ .... الْمَدْرَسَةِ.
الْبَاب	مَا هَذِه؟ هَذِهِ ....
ذَهَبَ	مَاذَا ....سَعِيد؟
هَذَا	.... الْوَلَدُ النَّافِذَةَ.
الْمَلْعَبِ	.....................الْبَاب.
إِلَى	فَتَحَ سَمِيرٌ ....
يَفْعَلُ	مَا هَذَا؟ ....بَيْتٌ.
النَّافِذَةَ	ذَهَبَ الْوَلَدُ إِلَى ....

Write Imperative verbs

masculine *singular*	Sit!	....	masculine *singular*	Get off!	....
feminine *singular*	Sit!	....	feminine *singular*	Get off!	....
plural *masculine*	Sit!	....	plural *masculine*	Get off!	....

Write in the missing words

هُوَ	هُوَ يَجْلِسُ .... الْكُرْسِيِّ.
الْكُرْسِيِّ	.... مُحَمَّدٌ حَقِيبَةً.
نَزَلَ	أَيْنَ الْوَلَدُ؟ هُوَ .... الْحَدِيقَةِ.
حَقِيبَةً	أَيْنَ أَحْمَدُ؟ .... فِي الْحَدِيقَةِ.
عَلَى	هُوَ .... الْمَلَابِسَ.
يَجْلِسُ	اِجْلِسِي عَلَى ....
أَيْنَ	.... التِّلْمِيذُ مِنَ الْحَافِلَةِ.
يَحْمِلُ	أَيْنَ الْبِنْتُ؟ .... فِي الْحَدِيقَةِ.
فِي	يَحْمِلُ أَحْمَدُ............
الْحَدِيقَةِ	............التِّلْمِيذُ عَلَى الْكُرْسِيِّ.
الْوَلَدُ	.... الْحَقِيبَةُ؟ هِيَ عَلَى الْكُرْسِيِّ.
هِيَ	ذَهَبَ مُحَمَّدٌ إِلَى ....
يَغْسِلُ	يَحْمِلُ .... الْكِتَابَ.

Write Imperative verbs

masculine *singular*	Go out!	....	masculine *singular*	Enter!	....
feminine *singular*	Go out!	....	feminine *singular*	Enter!	....
plural *masculine*	Go out!	....	plural *masculine*	Enter!	....

Write in the missing words

خَرَجَ	يَكْتُبُ بِلَالٌ ....
بَعِيدًا	هُوَ يَسْكُنُ ....مِنَ الْمَدْرَسَةِ.
بِ	.... مُحَمَّدٌ مِنَ الصَّفِّ.
الصَّفِّ	.... كَرِيمٌ قَرِيبًا مِنَ الْمَدْرَسَةِ.
مَعَ	هُوَ يَكْتُبُ عَلَى ....
يَكْتُبُ	...........................التِّلْمِيذُ إِلَى الصَّفِّ.
رِسَالَةً	هُوَ يَسْكُنُ...........................عَنِ الْمَدْرَسَةِ.
قَرِيبًا	هُوَ يَكْتُبُ ..... الْقَلَمِ.
الْقَلَمِ	دَخَلَ أَحْمَدُ إِلَى ....
دَخَلَ	هُوَ خَرَجَ...........................بِلَال.
مِنَ	دَخَلَ مُحَمَّدٌ إِلَى ....
يَسْكُنُ	كَتَبَ الْوَلَدُ بِ ....
الْغُرْفَةِ	خَرَجَ سَمِيرٌ...........................الْبَيْتِ.
الْوَرَقَةِ	...........................الْوَلَدُ عَلَى الْوَرَقَةِ.

Write Imperative verbs

masculine *singular*	Wear, Put on!	....	masculine *singular*	Drink!	....
feminine *singular*	Wear, Put on!	....	feminine *singular*	Drink!	....
plural *masculine*	Wear, Put on!	....	plural *masculine*	Drink!	....

Write in the missing words

يَلْبَسُ	يَلْعَبُ مُنِيرٌ بِ ....
دَرَّاجَةً	.... رَفِيقٌ حَلِيبًا.
يَرْكَبُ	يَلْبَسُ كَمَالٌ ....
أَبِي	يَرْكَبُ سَمِيرٌ ....
يَشْرَبُ	.... بِلَالٌ قَمِيصًا.
مَنْ	هُوَ .... بِاللُّعْبَةِ.
لُعْبَتِي	يَرْكَبُ أَحْمَدُ ....
حَلِيبًا	مَنْ هَذَا؟ هَذَا ....
قَمِيصًا	هُوَ .... حَافِلَةً.
حَافِلَةً	يَشْرَبُ عَلِيٌّ ....
يَلْعَبُ	.... هَذِهِ؟ هَذِهِ أُمِّي.

Write Imperative verbs

masculine singular	Finish, Complete!	....	masculine singular	Catch, Hold!	....
feminine singular	Finish, Complete!	....	feminine singular	Catch, Hold!	....
plural masculine	Finish, Complete!	....	plural masculine	Catch, Hold!	....

Write in the missing words

أَمْسَكَ	هُوَ أَغْلَقَ ....
تَحْتَ	أَكْمَلَ بِلَالٌ ....
عَلَى	الْكِتَابُ ....الطَّاوِلَةِ.
الْكُرَةَ	....................أَحْمَدُ الْكُرَةَ.
أَغْلَقَ	أَيْنَ قَلَمُكَ؟ هُوَ .... الْحَقِيبَةِ.
هِيَ	الْكُرَةُ ....الطَّاوِلَةِ.
أَكْمَلَ	أَغْلَقَ الْوَلَدُ ....
الْبَابَ	السَّيَّارَةُ .... الْجِسْرِ.
فِي	أَمْسَكَ التِّلْمِيذُ ....
الْوَاجِبَ	....................مَحْمُودٌ الدَّرْسَ.
التِّلْمِيذُ	أَيْنَ كُرَتُكَ؟ .... فِي السَّيَّارَةِ.
فَوْقَ	....................التِّلْمِيذُ النَّافِذَةَ.
النَّافِذَةَ	أَكْمَلَ ....الدَّرْسَ.

Write Imperative verbs

masculine *singular*	Work hard!	....	masculine *singular*	Smile!	....
feminine *singular*	Work hard!	....	feminine *singular*	Smile!	....
plural *masculine*	Work hard!	....	plural *masculine*	Smile!	....

Write in the missing words

مِنَ	ابْتَسَمَ ....
الْبَابَ	أَنَا .... مَالِيزِيَة.
هُوَ	يَجْتَهِدُ سَمِيرٌ فِي ....
سُورِيَة	أَيْنَ قَلَمُكِ؟ .... تَحْتَ الْكِتَابِ.
يَنْتَظِرُ	.... مُحَمَّدٌ الْأَصْدِقَاءَ.
الْكُرْسِيِّ	أَغْلَقَ الرَّجُلُ ....
يَجْتَهِدُ	يَسْكُنُ الْمُعَلِّمُ قَرِيبًا ....الْمَدْرَسَةِ.
اسْمُكَ	أَنَا مِنْ ....
صَدِيقِي	.... أَحْمَدُ فِي الدُّرُوسِ.
الْمَدْرَسَةِ	جَلَسَ الرَّجُلُ عَلَى ....
الدُّرُوسِ	مَا ....؟ اسْمِي بِلَال.
مِنْ	ذَهَبَ صَدِيقِي إِلَى ....

Write Imperative verbs

masculine *singular*	Welcome!	....	masculine *singular*	Use!	....
feminine *singular*	Welcome!	....	feminine *singular*	Use!	....
plural *masculine*	Welcome!	....	plural *masculine*	Use!	....

Write in the missing words

الدَّرَّاجَةَ	اِسْتَقْبَلَ الْمُعَلِّمُ ....
حَلِيبًا	..............عَبْدُ اللهِ مُبَكِّرًا.
الْأَخْضَرَ	اِسْتَعْمَلَ بَشِيرٌ الْقَلَمَ ....
الصَّفْرَاءُ	يَرْكَبُ أَخُوكَ ....
اِسْتَقْبَلَ	يَكْتُبُ أَبُوكَ ....
التَّلَامِيذَ	..............سَمِيرٌ مُتَأَخِّرًا.
اِسْتَيْقَظَ	اِسْتَيْقَظَ عَبْدُ اللهِ ....
الرِّسَالَةَ	اِسْتَعْمَلَ سَمِيرٌ اللَّوْنَ ....
يَسْتَيْقِظُ	يَشْرَبُ أَخُوكَ ....
الْأَزْرَقَ	..............الْمُعَلِّمُ التَّلَامِيذَ.
مُبَكِّرًا	يَجْلِسُ أَبُوكِ فِي ....
الْحَدِيقَةِ	أَيْنَ الْحَافِلَةُ ....؟

Write Imperative verbs

masculine *singular*	Arrange, Organize!	....	masculine *singular*	Think!	....
feminine *singular*	Arrange, Organize!	....	feminine *singular*	Think!	....
plural *masculine*	Arrange, Organize!	....	plural *masculine*	Think!	....

Write in the missing words

عَلِيٌّ	...................سَلِيمٌ أَسْنَانَهُ.
وَرَاءَ	هُوَ يُرَتِّبُ ....
هِيَ	يُفَكِّرُ حَسَنٌ فِي الذَّهَابِ إِلَى ....
الشَّجَرَةِ	الْكُرَةُ...................الصُّنْدُوقِ.
حَقِيبَتَهُ	يُنَظِّفُ ....أَسْنَانَهُ.
الْهَدِيَّةَ	الْكُرَةُ...................الصُّنْدُوقِ.
أَسْنَانَهُ	يُرَتِّبُ الْوَلَدُ ....
غُرْفَتَهُ	يَسْتَيْقِظُ مُنِيرٌ مُبَكِّرًا وَيُنَظِّفُ ....
الْحَدِيقَةِ	فَتَحَ مُحَمَّدٌ ....وَابْتَسَمَ.
أَمَامَ	الْوَلَدُ وَرَاءَ ....
نَظَّفَ	أَيْنَ كُرَتُهُ؟ ....أَمَامَ الصُّنْدُوقِ.

Write Imperative verbs

masculine *singular*	Stop!	....	masculine *singular*	Learn!	....
feminine *singular*	Stop!	....	feminine *singular*	Learn!	....
plural *masculine*	Stop!	....	plural *masculine*	Learn!	....

Write in the missing words

الْمَكْتَب	هُوَ يَتَكَلَّمُ اللُّغَةَ ....
الْمُعَلِّمُ	ذَهَبَ سَمِيرٌ إِلَى ....
قَلِيلًا	يَتَعَلَّمُ التِّلْمِيذُ الْقِرَاءَةَ وَالْكِتَابَةَ فِي ....
يَتَكَلَّمُ	تَوَقَّفَ .... أَمَامَ الْمَدْرَسَةِ.
مَعَ	الْكِتَابُ فَوْقَ ....
الْمَكْتَبَةِ	يَتَعَلَّمُ بِلَالٌ .... فِي الْمَدْرَسَةِ.
الْكِتَابَةَ	أَيْنَ كِتَابُهَا؟ .... عَلَى الْمَكْتَبِ.
الْعَرَبِيَّةَ	تَكَلَّمْ .... الْمُعَلِّمِ اللُّغَةَ الْعَرَبِيَّةَ.
الْمَدْرَسَةِ	.... الْمُعَلِّمُ اللُّغَةَ الْعَرَبِيَّةَ.
الْقِرَاءَةَ	هُوَ يَتَكَلَّمُ اللُّغَةَ الْعَرَبِيَّةَ ....
هُوَ	يَتَعَلَّمُ التِّلْمِيذُ الْقِرَاءَةَ وَ .... فِي الْمَدْرَسَةِ.

Write Imperative verbs

masculine *singular*	Revise!	....	masculine *singular*	Travel!	....
feminine *singular*	Revise!	....	feminine *singular*	Travel!	....
plural *masculine*	Revise!	....	plural *masculine*	Travel!	....

Write in the missing words

سَافَرَ	............الْوَلَدُ أُمَّهَا.
طَائِرَةِ	............أَحْمَدُ دُرُوسَهُ.
الرَّحْمَان	............أَبِي مَعَ صَدِيقِهِ إِلَى الْمَدِينَةِ بِالقِطَارِ.
يُسَاعِدُ	سَافَرَ رَفِيقٌ إِلَى بَلَدِهِ بِ............
أَسْنَانَهُ	يَسْكُنُ أَبِي فِي ....
يُرَاجِعُ	رَاجَعَ التِّلْمِيذُ سُورَةَ ....
قَرْيَةٍ	تَعَلَّمَ سَمِيرٌ ....فِي الْمَدْرَسَةِ.
سُورَةَ	تَوَقَّفَتِ السَّيَّارَةُ ....الشَّجَرَةِ.
اللُّغَةَ الْعَرَبِيَّةَ	يُنَظِّفُ سَلِيمٌ ....
حَقِيبَتَهُ	يَتَكَلَّمُ الْمُعَلِّمُ مَعَ ....
أَمَامَ	رَاجِعْ .... النَّاس.
أُمِّي	يُرَتِّبُ رَفِيقٌ ....

Write Imperative verbs

masculine *singular*	Arrive!	....	masculine *singular*	Find!	....
feminine *singular*	Arrive!	....	feminine *singular*	Find!	....
plural *masculine*	Arrive!	....	plural *masculine*	Find!	....

Write in the missing words

فِي الْحَقِيبَةِ	وَضَعَ التِّلْمِيذُ الْكِتَابَ عَلَى ....
وَرَاءَ	وَقَفَ ....أَمَامَ الْمَدْرَسَةِ.
وَصَلَ	ذَهَبَ الطَّالِبُ إِلَى ....
لُعْبَةً	..............سَمِيرٌ قَلَمِي.
الْمَكْتَبِ	وَضَعَ الطِّفْلُ الْقَلَمَ ....
مَحَطَّةِ الْقِطَارِ	.... حَسَنٌ إِلَى الْمَطَارِ مُبَكِّرًا.
الْمُعَلِّمُ	هُوَ وَجَدَ ....فِي الْمَلْعَبِ.
وَجَدَ	ضَعْ الْكُرْسِي .... الْغُرْفَةِ.
الْمَكْتَبَةِ	وَصَلَ صَدِيقِي إِلَى ....
فِي	وَقَفَ الْوَلَدُ .... الْبَابِ.

Write Imperative verbs

masculine *singular*	Visit!	....	masculine *singular*	Return!	....
feminine *singular*	Visit!	....	feminine *singular*	Return!	....
plural *masculine*	Visit!	....	plural *masculine*	Return!	....

Write in the missing words

سَيَّارَةٌ	قَالَ سَمِيرٌ: لِي ....
الْمَدْرَسَةِ	زَارَ الْوَلَدُ ....
قَالَ	قَالَ خَالِدٌ: عِنْدِي ....
أَخٌ	عَادَ مَحْمُودٌ مِنَ ....
عِنْدِي	مَاذَا ....أَحْمَد؟
لِي	....................خَالِي إِلَى الْمَطَارِ.
اِسْمُهَا	قَالَ الْمُعَلِّمُ: ....قَلَمٌ وَكُرَّاسَةٌ.
وَصَلَ	لَدَيَّ أُسْرَةٌ ....
عَمَّهُ	لَهَا أُخْتٌ. .... نَادِيَة.
كَبِيرَةٌ	....................أَخٌ وَثَلَاثَةُ أَخَوَاتٍ.

Write Imperative verbs

masculine *singular*	Fly!	....	masculine *singular*	Live!	....
feminine *singular*	Fly!	....	feminine *singular*	Live!	....
plural *masculine*	Fly!	....	plural *masculine*	Live!	....

Write in the missing words

الْمَدِينَةِ	يَبِيعُ خَالِدٌ ....في السُّوقِ.
أَخٌ	تَطِيرُ ....فَوْقَ الْبَلَدِ.
أَعِنْدَكَ	هَلْ عِنْدَكَ دَرَّاجَةٌ يَا أَخِي؟ نَعَم، .... دَرَّاجَةٌ.
يَعِيشُ	يَعِيشُ مُحَمَّدٌ فِي ....
فَوَاكِهَ	...............أَبِي سَيَّارَتَهُ.
عِنْدِي	هَلْ لَهُ ....؟
يَبِيعُ	...............جَدِّي فِي الْقَرْيَةِ.
السُّوقِ	أَلَكِ أُخْتٌ؟ نَعَم، .... أُخْتٌ وَاحِدَةٌ.
الطَّائِرَةُ	...............قَلَمٌ؟
لِي	يَبِيعُ عَمِّي عِنَبَ وَتُفَّاحَ فِي ....

Write Imperative verbs

masculine *singular*	Be afraid of!	....	masculine *singular*	Get!	....
feminine *singular*	Be afraid of!	....	feminine *singular*	Get!	....
plural *masculine*	Be afraid of!	....	plural *masculine*	Get!	....

Write in the missing words

أُخْتٌ	.... الطِّفْلُ مُبَكِّرًا.
السَّرِيرِ	.... الْفِيلُ مِنَ الْفَأْرِ.
نَالَ	هَلْ لَكِ أُخْتٌ؟ لَا، لَيْسَ لِي ....
الْجَائِزَةَ	يَنَامُ الْوَلَدُ عَلَى ....
خَافَ	هَلْ عِنْدَهَا سَيَّارَةٌ؟ لَا، لَيْسَ .... سَيَّارَةٌ.
نَامَ	.... بِلَالٌ الْجَائِزَةَ.
لَيْسَ	أَنَا أَخَافُ مِنَ ....
عِنْدَهَا	هَلْ لَهُ أَخٌ؟ لَا، لَيْسَ .... أَخٌ.
الْأَسَدِ	زَارَ التَّلَامِيذُ ....
لَهُ	نَالَ التِّلْمِيذُ .... فِي الْمَدْرَسَةِ.
حَدِيقَةَ الْحَيَوَانِ	هَلْ عِنْدَكَ كُرَةٌ؟ لَا، .... عِنْدِي كُرَةٌ.

Write Imperative verbs

masculine *singular*	Build!	....	masculine *singular*	Buy!	....
feminine *singular*	Build!	....	feminine *singular*	Buy!	....
plural *masculine*	Build!	....	plural *masculine*	Buy!	....

Write in the missing words

الْمَسَاءِ	بَنَى خَالِدٌ ....
عِنْدِي	.... أَخِي كَثِيرًا.
بِصَدِيقِهِ	هُوَ .... إِلَى بَيْتِهِ.
قَصْرًا	.....................الْوَلَدُ قَلَمًا وَدَفْتَرًا مِنَ السُّوقِ.
الصَّبَاحِ	هُوَ يَرْتَدِي ....
يَبْكِي	مَا كَانَ .... وَقْتٌ.
لِ	اِلْتَقَى أَحْمَدُ ....فِي الْمَدِينَةِ.
جَرَى	ذَهَبَ أَبِي إِلَى السُّوقِ فِي ....
لِأُمِّهِ	يَبْنِي أَبِي الْمَنْزِلَ .... الْقَرْيَةِ.
قَمِيصًا	هُوَ اِشْتَرَى دَفْتَرًا .... صَدِيقِهِ.
فِي	كَتَبَ رَفِيقٌ الرِّسَالَةَ ....
اِشْتَرَى	هُوَ اِلْتَقَى بِأَصْدِقَائِهِ فِي ....

Write Imperative verbs

masculine *singular*	Forget!	....	masculine *singular*	Stay!	....
feminine *singular*	Forget!	....	feminine *singular*	Stay!	....
plural *masculine*	Forget!	....	plural *masculine*	Stay!	....

Write in the missing words

مِنَ	يَبْقَى أَحْمَدُ فِي ....
نَسِيَ	نَسِيَ .... كُرَتَهُ.
كَثِيرًا	خَافَ الْكَلْبُ .... الْقِطَّةِ.
قَرْيَتِهِ	يَلْبَسُ مُحَمَّدٌ ....الشِّتَاءِ.
فَصْلِ	..............أَحْمَدُ فِي بَيْتِهِ.
الْوَلَدُ	يَرْتَدِي بِلَالٌ مَلَابِسَ ....
يَبْقَى	هُوَ يَنْسَى ....
عِنْدِي	يَنَامُ دُبٌّ فِي .... الشِّتَاءِ.
الصَّيْف	هَلْ عِنْدَكَ مِظَلَّةٌ؟ نَعَم، .... مِظَلَّةٌ.
مَلَابِسَ	..............التِّلْمِيذُ الْكِتَابَ.

71

Write Imperative verbs

masculine *singular*	Recite!	....	masculine *singular*	Call, invite!	....
feminine *singular*	Recite!	....	feminine *singular*	Call, invite!	....
plural *masculine*	Recite!	....	plural *masculine*	Call, invite!	....

Write in the missing words

صَدِيقَهُ	تَلَا عَبْدُ الله .... النَّاس.
سُورَةَ	هُوَ سَمِعَ .... في الْغَابَةِ.
تَلَا	بَيْتٌ ....
الرَّحْمَان	دَعَا سَلِيمٌ .... إِلَى بَيْتِهِ.
كَبِيرٌ	صُورَةٌ ....
دَعَا	.... بِلَالٌ الضَّيْفَ إِلَى بَيْتِهِ.
إِلَى اللهِ	.... الإِمَامُ سُورَةَ الرَّحْمَان.
جَمِيلَةٌ	.... جَيِّدٌ.
الصَّوْتَ	دَعَا مُحَمَّدٌ ....
مُعَلِّمٌ	يَتْلُو خَالِدٌ سُورَةَ ....

Write Imperative verbs

masculine *singular*	Name!	....	masculine *singular*	Pray!	....
feminine *singular*	Name!	....	feminine *singular*	Pray!	....
plural *masculine*	Name!	....	plural *masculine*	Pray!	....

Write in the missing words

صَلَّى	يُصَلِّي بِلَالٌ فِي ....
سَمَّى	صَلَّى أَخِي صَلَاةَ .... فِي الْمَسْجِدِ.
الْمَسْجِد	.... الْوَلَدُ كَلْبَهُ بوُب.
الْجَدِيد	هُوَ .... صَلَاةَ الْعَصْرِ فِي الْمَسْجِدِ.
ذَهَب	.... الْوَلَدُ الصُّنْدُوقَ الْكَبِيرَ.
صَلَوَاتٍ	.... أَبِي إِلَى الْمَسْجِدِ.
عَائِشَةً	بَاعَ كَرِيمٌ .... الْقَدِيمَ.
الْمَغْرِب	يُصَلِّي الْمُسْلِمُ خَمْسَ .... كُلَّ يَوْمٍ.
الْمَكْتَب	سَمَّى أَبٌ اِبْنَتَهُ ....
فَتَح	صَلَّى أَحْمَدُ صَلَاةَ الْعِشَاءِ فِي الْمَسْجِدِ ....

Write Imperative verbs

masculine *singular*	Throw!	....	masculine *singular*	Give!	....
feminine *singular*	Throw!	....	feminine *singular*	Give!	....
plural *masculine*	Throw!	....	plural *masculine*	Give!	....

Write in the missing words

يَشْرَبُ	...............الْوَلَدُ كُرَةً فِي السَّلَّةِ.
أَعْطَى	هُوَ أَعْطَى الْكِتَابَ ....
الطِّفْلُ	...............مُحَمَّدٌ عَصِيرًا.
هَذِهِ	هَذَا رَأْسٌ وَ............... فَمٌّ.
أَلْقَى	هُوَ أَلْقَى ....فِي الْمَاءِ.
أَعْطِنِي	...............صَالِحٌ سَيَّارَةً لِصَدِيقِهِ.
هَذَا	أَعْطِنِي .... مِنَ الشَّايِ.
لِلْمُعَلِّمَةِ	قَالَ .... : أَعْطِنِي حَلْوَى.
سَمَكَةً	...............كَأْسَ الْمَاءِ.
كُوبًا	هَذِهِ يَدٌ و............... أُذُنٌ.

Write Imperative verbs

masculine *singular*	See!	....	masculine *singular*	Come, Bring!	....
feminine *singular*	See!	....	feminine *singular*	Come, Bring!	....
plural *masculine*	See!	....	plural *masculine*	Come, Bring!	....

Write in the missing words

بَعْدَ	يَأْتِي فَصْلُ الرَّبِيعُ بَعْدَ ....
كَبِيرَةً	هُوَ .... أَرْنَبًا.
الدُّرُوسِ	جَاءَتِ الْحَافِلَةُ ....
مُحَمَّدٌ	هُوَ ذَهَبَ إِلَى مَكَّةِ الْمُكَرَّمَةِ قَبْلَ ....
فَصْلِ الشِّتَاءِ	هُوَ تَكَلَّمَ مَعَ الْمُعَلِّمِ .... الدَّرسِ.
يَأْتِي	رَأَى الْوَلَدُ طَائِرَةً ....
أُسْبُوع	.... سَمِيرٌ إِلَى بَلَدِهِ قَبْلَ عَامٍ.
رَأَى	اِلْتَقَى بِلَالٌ مَعَ أَصْدِقَائِهِ بَعْدَ ....
مُتَأَخِّرَةً	.... عِيدُ الْفِطْرِ بَعْدَ شَهْرِ رَمَضَانَ.
ذَهَبَ	زَارَ .... أُخْتَهُ قَبْلَ أُسْبُوعٍ.

Write Imperative verbs

masculine *singular*	Smell!	....	masculine *singular*	Count!	....
feminine *singular*	Smell!	....	feminine *singular*	Count!	....
plural *masculine*	Smell!	....	plural *masculine*	Count!	....

Write in the missing words

الْأَحْجَارَ	....................بِلَالٌ رَائِحَةَ الزُّهُورِ.
قَرِيبًا	يَشُمُّ صَالِحٌ ....
هُوَ	أَيْنَ كِتَابُ .... ؟ هُوَ عَلَى الْمَكْتَبِ.
جَمِيلًا	هُوَ .... : وَاحِد، اِثْنَان، ثَلَاثَة، أَرْبَعَة...
شَمَّ	يَسْكُنُ جَدِّي .... مِنَ الْجِبَالِ.
الصَّفِّ	يَعُدُّ الْوَلَدُ ....
مُحَمَّدٍ	أَيْنَ .... السَّيَّارَةِ؟ هُوَ عَلَى الطَّاوِلَةِ.
زَهْرَةً	وَجَدَ كَرِيمٌ حَجَرًا .... فِي الْبَحْرِ.
يَعُدُّ	يَعُدُّ الْمُعَلِّمُ التَّلَامِيذَ فِي ....
مِفْتَاحُ	أَيْنَ اِبْنُ بِلَالٍ؟ .... فِي الْمَدْرَسَةِ.

Write Imperative verbs

masculine *singular*	Prepare!	....	masculine *singular*	Love, Like!	....
feminine *singular*	Prepare!	....	feminine *singular*	Love, Like!	....
plural *masculine*	Prepare!	....	plural *masculine*	Love, Like!	....

Write in the missing words

يُعِدُّ	...............أَحْمَدُ عَائِلَتَهُ.
كُلَّ يَوْمٍ	يَجْلِسُ الْكَلْبُ تَحْتَ ....
الطِّفْلُ	يَشْرَبُ مُنِيرٌ حَلِيبًا .... مَسَاءٍ.
الْمَطْبَخِ	...............سَمِيرٌ الْفُطُورَ فِي الْمَطْبَخِ.
الْمَائِدَةِ	جَلَسَتِ الْعَائِلَةُ .... الْمَائِدَةِ.
كُلَّ	يُحِبُّ إِبْرَاهِيمُ تَعَلُّمَ .... الْعَرَبِيَّةِ.
يُحِبُّ	يُحِبُّ .... أُمَّهُ.
الْفُطُورَ	هُوَ يُعِدُّ الْعَشَاءَ فِي ....
حَوْلَ	يَذْهَبُ أَبِي إِلَى السُّوقِ ....
اللُّغَةِ	هُوَ يُعِدُّ .... كُلَّ صَبَاحٍ.

Write Imperative verbs

masculine *singular*	Take!	....	masculine *singular*	Eat!
feminine *singular*	Take!	....	feminine *singular*	Eat!
plural *masculine*	Take!	....	plural *masculine*	Eat!

Write in the missing words

سَأَلَ	.........بِلَالٌ فِي الْمَطْعَمِ الْبَارِحَةِ.
خُبْزًا	أَخَذَ هِشَامٌ ....مِنْ حَقِيبَتِهِ.
جِدًّا	أَكَلَ حَسَنٌ فِي الْمَطْعَمِ ....
جَيِّدٌ	.........الْمُعَلِّمُ التِّلْمِيذَ السُّؤَالَ.
أَكَلَ	يَأْكُلُ كَرِيمٌ ....كُلَّ صَبَاحٍ.
الْبَارِحَةِ	.........الْفَوَاكِهَ كُلَّ يَوْمٍ.
أَخَذَ	.........التِّلْمِيذُ كِتَابًا كُلَّ يَوْمٍ.
قَلَمًا	قَالَ الْمُعَلِّمُ: هَذَا سُؤَالٌ ....
يَقْرَأُ	.........الْوَلَدُ كُرَةً مِنَ الصُّنْدُوقِ.
كُلُوا	هَذَا صَغِيرٌ ....

Write Imperative verbs

masculine *singular*	Hunt!	....	masculine *singular*	Choose!	....
feminine *singular*	Hunt!	....	feminine *singular*	Choose!	....
plural *masculine*	Hunt!	....	plural *masculine*	Choose!	....

Write in the missing words

فَرَاشَةً	يَحْتَاجُ .... إِلَى سَيَّارَةٍ.
الْأَحْمَرَ	............صَالِحٌ سَمَكًا.
جَيِّدَةٌ	الصُّنْدُوقُ ....
وَقْتٍ	يَنَامُ الطِّفْلُ فِي ....
أَبِي	............كَرِيمٌ إِلَى مِسْطَرَةٍ.
اللَّيْلِ	اِخْتَارَ كَرِيمٌ الْقَلَمَ ....
كَبِيرٌ	الْمُعَلِّمَةُ............
يَخْتَارُ	اِصْطَادَ طَارِقٌ ....
يَصْطَادُ	هُوَ يَحْتَاجُ إِلَى ....
يَحْتَاجُ	هُوَ ....اللُّعْبَةَ ثُمَّ يَلْعَبُ بِهَا.

Write Imperative verbs

masculine *singular*	Obey!	....	masculine *singular*	Answer!	....
feminine *singular*	Obey!	....	feminine *singular*	Answer!	....
plural *masculine*	Obey!	....	plural *masculine*	Answer!	....

Write in the missing words

يُطِيعُ	.... حَسَنٌ عَلَى السُّؤَالِ.
الْفَجْرِ	يُطِيعُ الْوَلَدُ ....
يَوْمُ	ذَهَبَ سَمِيرٌ إِلَى الْمَطْعَمِ يَوْمُ ....
الْمَطْعَمِ	.... الْأَوْلَادُ الذَّهَابَ إِلَى الْحَدِيقَةِ.
أَجَابَ	اِشْتَرَى بِلَالٌ .... جَدِيدَةً.
وَالِدَيْهِ	هُوَ صَلَّى صَلَاةَ ....
اِلْتَقَى	ذَهَبَ أَبِي إِلَى السُّوقِ .... الْأَحَد.
أَرَادَ	الْمُسْلِمُ .... اللّه.
سَاعَةً	أَكَلَ كَرِيمٌ فِي .... يَوْمُ الْخَمِيسِ.
السَّبْت	.... أَحْمَدُ بِصَدِيقِهِ يَوْمُ الثُّلَاثَاء.

Countries

Afghanistan	أَفْغَانِسْتَان	Saudi Arabia	السَّعُودِيَّة
Pakistan	بَاكِسْتَان	Kuwait	الكُوَيْت
Bangladesh	بَنْغَلَادِيش	Iraq	العِرَاق
Malaysia	مَاليزِيَة	Jordan	الأُرْدُنّ
Indonesia	إِنْدونِيسِيَة	Emirates	الإِمَارَات
Nigeria	نَيْجِيرِيَة	Qatar	قَطَر
Senegal	السِنْغَال	Oman	عُمَان
Kenya	كِينِيَة	Egypt	مِصْر
India	الهِنْد	Yemen	اليَمَن
Britain	بَرِيطَانِيَة	Palestine	فِلَسْطِين
England	إِنْكِلْتَرَة	Syria	سُورِيَة
America	أَمْرِيكَة	Lebanon	لُبْنَان
Canada	كَنَدَا	Sudan	السُّودَان
Australia	أُسْتِرَالِيَة	Algeria	الجَزَائِر
China	الصِّين	Morocco	المَغْرِب
Japan	اليَابَان	Tunisia	تُونُس
France	فَرَنْسَة	Somalia	الصُّومَال
		Turkey	تُرْكِيَّة
		Iran	إِيرَان

81

Printed in Great Britain
by Amazon

55955108R00048